Take a Break
1001 Top tips

WELCOME

Who doesn't love a helpful tip or clever hack to make life easier? Every week at Take 5 we're sent hundreds of handy tips and tricks from our lovely readers all across Australia, so we've compiled 1001 of your wonderful – and sometimes wacky! – suggestions in one ultimate easy-to-use guide of home hints.

You'll find everything from gardening pointers to make your lawn the envy of the neighbourhood, simple fashion and beauty advice, money-saving mantras, travelling tricks, to the downright wackiest tips we've ever received (pitta pocket purse, anyone?).

The Take 5 team have had a lot of fun compiling this book, and there's been many a conversation in the office after someone has tried out one of the weirder inclusions. My personal favourite – cleaning the glass of your combustion fireplace with ash (it really works!).

These 1001 tried-and-tested tips from Take 5 magazine readers are all about making *your* life easier, and we're sure it's a book you'll refer to time and time again!

Dani

CONTENTS

PICTURES: ISTOCK TAKE 5 ACCEPTS READERS' TIPS IN GOOD FAITH. HOWEVER, TAKE 5 CANNOT ASSURE READERS THAT THEY WILL BE EFFECTIVE IN ALL CASES OR BE RESPONSIBLE FOR ANY RESULTING LOSS OR DAMAGE.

KITCHEN/COOKING	6
LAUNDRY	38
STAIN REMOVAL	50
CLEANING	62
INDOOR LIVING	88
TRAVEL	106
FASHION/BEAUTY	116
THE GREAT OUTDOORS	138
MONEY SAVING	156
PETS	174
OFFICE/GIFTS/CRAFT	184
KIDS	198
HOME REMEDIES	220
INDEX	229

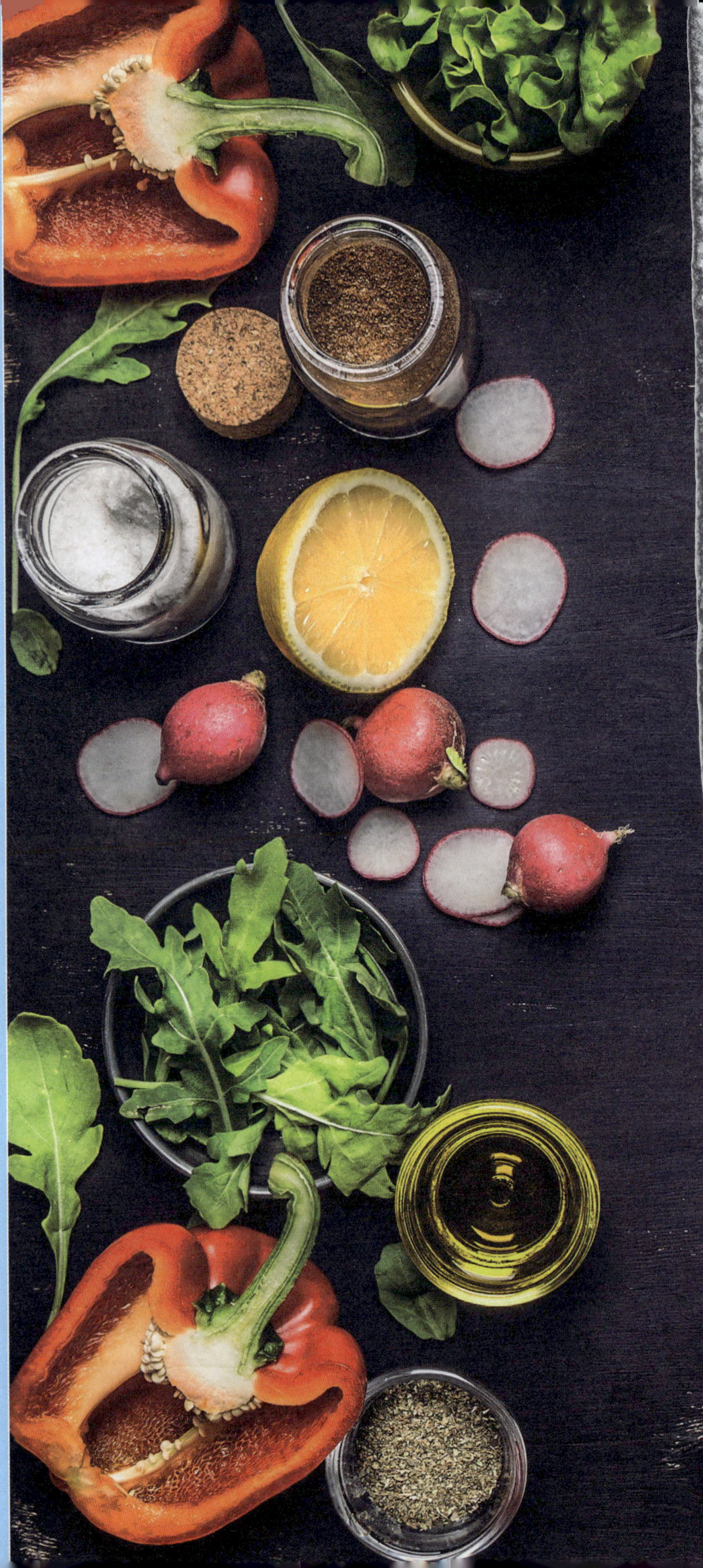

KITCHEN /COOKING

KITCHEN /COOKING

- When you've finished with your cake tins and muffin trays, wash them immediately and return to the warm, turned-off oven. It will dry them thoroughly to prevent rust and other marks.
Kay Sweeney, Fyshwick, ACT.

- To keep soft drinks fizzier for longer place an upside down teaspoon into the drink.
Sophie Gofton, Quinns Rock, WA.

- Beating butter and sugar together while baking can be a difficult process. I simply dip my beaters in hot water and I find they mix the ingredients much smoother that way!
Lucy Coode, Orange, NSW.

- I keep a magnifying glass in an easy-to-reach place in the kitchen. Products often have such tiny writing that I find I'm always needing one.
Paige McBurney, Sinnamon Park, Qld.

- Having trouble getting bottle lids off? They're much easier to screw off when you're wearing rubber gloves.
Kathy Simpson, via email.

- When you need to crush biscuits for a recipe and don't have access to a blender, a clean meat mallet works well. Press gently over a couple at a time, until they are to the consistency you want. Works a treat.
K.Knight, Victoria Point, Qld.

KATHLEEN TRIES IT OUT!

WACKY BUT IT WORKS

If your kids love making pancakes for breakfast but always make such a mess, store your batter in a tomato sauce bottle. It's easy for them to pour out and shortens the wash up, too!

- You can make your potatoes last longer by storing them with an apple in the mix. They won't soften or bud nearly as fast!
Lucy Williams, Perth, WA.

- Bread when frozen often gets a layer of frost on it. To eliminate this, simply wrap the bread in a second bag. A plastic shopping bags work best. Frozen bread will last for several weeks.
Leann Middlemass, Burnley, Vic.

- If you buy bananas at the weekend, write the days of the week on them in order of ripeness so you're not left with black ones at the end of the week.
R. Owen, Helensvale, Qld.

- The easiest way to line a cake tin is to fold a piece of baking paper into four and place the tip in the centre of the tin. Tear away an arch, shaped from the inner rim of the baking tin and once unfolded it will reveal a perfect circle.
Alana Everard, Clarinda, Vic.

KITCHEN/COOKING

- For a healthy frozen treat, peel ripe bananas and push a paddle pop stick halfway into one end of each banana. Place in bags and pop into the freezer. They will keep for four weeks.
Peter Trees, Nambucca Heads, NSW.

- Make a pot of coffee and freeze in an ice-cube tray so when you make an iced coffee it doesn't get watered down.
Annie Crawford, Bondi, NSW.

- Soak bamboo sticks in water for at least 15 minutes before making your kebabs to stop the wood burning on the barbecue.
Kylie Tweeddale, Australind, WA.

- If you're melting chocolate and it starts to harden, just stir in a drop of vegetable oil.
Ida Schroder, Victoria Point, Qld.

- To maintain moisture when cooking corn on the cob, wrap it in wet paper towel and zap in the microwave until cooked.
Lisbeth Hone, Young, NSW.

- Make an instant cupcake carrier by cutting crosses in a shoebox lid.
Bel Tcaciuc, Amphitheatre, Vic.

- A frozen saturated sponge in a zip-lock bag makes an icepack that won't drip all over when it melts.
Amanda Hubbard, Malvern, Vic.

- If you ever have leftover wine, don't pour it down the sink away. Freeze it into ice cubes for future use in casseroles, stews and sauces.
Kelli Baldwin, Tenterfield, NSW.

- Add a pinch of sugar when boiling corn on the cob. It will help bring out the corn's natural sweetness.
Dora Stevens, via email.

- If you have nowhere to put the wooden spoon when mixing a pot of food, put it in the part of the saucepan with the hole in the handle, so the sauce on the spoon doesn't go everywhere.
Benjamin Caldwell, Fitzroy, Vic.

- Stir grated cheese in to shop-bought coleslaw to quickly turn it into a delicious filing for jacket potatoes.
Glennys Galvin, Wynnum, Qld.

- To make BLTs, or any toasted sandwich, place two slices of bread in a single toaster slot. This way, the bread gets warm and toasty on the outside, but stays soft and chewy on the inside.
Claire Garcia, Chermside, Qld.

KITCHEN/COOKING

- Turn your muffin tray over and shape pastry over bases to make perfect tart shells. They bake in no time and are an ideal size.
Cath Burges, Bunbury, WA.

- Pop a bay leaf into flour or grain when storing them to deter weevils.
Ella Corcoran, Launceston, Tas.

- Make sure your cakes rise with a neat straight edge by extending your baking paper lining well over the sides of the tin.
Kylie Tweeddale, Australind, WA.

- When pouring juice from a carton, cut off both top corners so it doesn't 'glug' when pouring. The air is released making it much easier to pour.
Tracey Couch, Singleton, WA.

- Disinfect your kitchen sponge by rinsing in a solution of vinegar and water and microwaving on high for two minutes.
Chistine Ling, Carlton, Vic.

- Buy eggs when they're cheap and freeze them. Simply crack eggs open and freeze in an ice-cube tray. Once frozen, remove the eggs and place in a freezer bag.
Mary Cowan, Richmond, NSW.

- To prevent your pan from staining while boiling eggs, add a teaspoon of brown vinegar to the water.
Ingrid Cohen, North Bondi, NSW.

KATHLEEN TRIES IT OUT!

WACKY BUT IT WORKS

If you have cold hands, use a few tea bags to make hand warmers! Just pop a hot tea bag into a sandwich bag and tie a knot in the top to prevent leaks. They'll keep you warm for a long time.

- Ward off pantry moths by placing new packets of dry goods in the freezer for a few days. It'll kill off any eggs or larvae.
Glenys Smith, Gosford, NSW.

- Keep string shopping bags hanging on the kitchen doorknob for your dirty tea towels. When the time comes to clean up, just put everything together into the washing machine.
Margaret Ainslie, Sunshine, Vic.

- Spilled slimy raw egg? Sprinkle salt generously over the egg and wait for two minutes and then wipe it up. The salt makes it much easier.
Danielle Norton, Osborne Park, WA.

- When heating taco shells, hang them on the oven racks to warm them up much faster.
Suzie Prince, Fairfield, Vic.

KITCHEN/COOKING

- Smear petroleum jelly around the fridge seals every few months to keep them working longer.
Polly Barton, Darlinghurst, NSW.

- Wash out pop-top squeeze bottles from mayonnaise or sauce. They can be used to ice cakes.
Talya Sinn, Darwin, NT.

To ripen green tomatoes, put them in a box with a banana. They'll turn red in no time.
Therese Snowden, Newcastle, NSW.

- To remove odours from plastic containers, wet a piece of newspaper, put it in the container and leave in the freezer overnight. In the morning, the smell will be gone.
Patty Dehaven, Karatha, WA.

- When boiling carrots, pour some orange juice in the saucepan as it makes them sweeter and adds flavour.
Betty Gough, Charters Towers, Qld.

- Keep an eye dropper to use for food colouring. This way it's much easier to control how much you use.
Jess Racioppi, Birrong, NSW.

- Small glass fruit juice bottles can be used to store dried herbs and spices. They have airtight lids and don't take up a lot of space.
Leonie Mann, Carlton South, Vic.

- Rather than buying expensive vegetable cooking oils spray, buy cheaper olive or canola oil in bulk and pour it into a spray bottle from a bargain shop.
Janelle Babic, Scoresby, Vic.

- Instead of fishing around with your fingers to dig out broken egg shells from a bowl of cracked eggs, use one of the egg shell halves to scoop it out. Much easier.
Fatima Townsend, Yass, NSW.

- To prevent mould on fresh raspberries and strawberries, rinse them in a solution of one part cider vinegar to 10 parts water, drain on paper towel and store in the fridge.
Karina Grummell, Picton, NSW.

- To cut a cake in half – ready for a cream filling – put a piece of cotton thread around the cake, tie and pull. The cake will cut evenly and you won't have any crumbs.
Audrey Hickey, Laidley, Qld.

- If a recipe calls for caster sugar and you've run out, simply whizz ordinary sugar in the food processor for a few seconds.
Rose Conkling, Mildura, NSW.

- If you want to oven-cook a jacket potato quickly, push a metal skewer through it before baking. The skewer cooks the potato from the inside, taking less time. Don't try this in the microwave.
Jody Melton, Cooma, NSW.

- If you drop a can of soft drink or it gets shaken up, to keep it from exploding when you pop the top, use your thumb and middle finger to thump up and down on the side of the can as you rotate it for about 20 seconds, then you can pop the top and enjoy.
Eydie Cash, Goulburn, NSW.

- To get more juice from lemons, heat them briefly in the microwave before squeezing.
Leonora Thompson, Bendigo, Vic.

- Place a wet paper towel or damp tea towel under your chopping board to prevent it from sliding.
Katrina Greer, via email.

- Place wax paper over ice-cream before placing the lid on – it stops icy bits forming when in the freezer.
Nataly Vickerson, Milton, NSW.

- To remove the stem of a strawberry without cutting off a chunk of the top, push a straw through the bottom to the top. The stem will pop off.
Kate Kibby, Claremont, WA.

- When defrosting the freezer, I fill a spray bottle with hot water and spray the ice. It comes off very easily and the whole job is finished in about 15 minutes.
Netta Naidoo, Bligh Park, NSW.

- Keep a safety pin on the kitchen curtains to slip your rings onto when you're busy in the kitchen or washing up.
Alisha Baker, Deception Bay, Qld.

WACKY BUT IT WORKS

If you need to hem a dress but are short on time, just fold the material to the right length and secure with some heavy duty duct tape. You'll save money on a seamstress and no-one will never know!
Danielle Kirkwood, Sheffield, Tas.

KITCHEN/COOKING

- If you need a rolling pin and don't have one, try using a wine bottle instead. And if you're using it to roll out pasty, a chilled wine bottle gives great results.
Tina Baker, Goulburn, NSW.

- When cooking with sticky ingredients such as honey, dip your measuring spoon in flour, then shake it off. You'll find the honey will slide off more easily.
Candice Thompson, Bellbird, NSW.

- Don't throw out overripe bananas – simply mash and freeze them. They are great for baking.
Tracey Couch, Singleton, WA.

- I discovered that just a quick dash of cold water on custard prevents that yucky 'skin' from forming on top.
Lisa Hibberts, Mount Victoria, NSW.

- Make your own icing sugar. Blend ordinary sugar in a blender until it turns into soft 'icing' sugar.
Vicki Wong, Leichhardt, NSW.

- Always keep a few empty soft drink bottles or large jars under the kitchen sink so you can dispose of used oil properly – it's far better than just pouring the oil down the sink.
Mary Maucher, Orelia, WA.

- Cockroaches and silverfish will disappear if you sprinkle Epsom salts under your fridge and around the cupboard and pantry shelves. It's much cheaper than commercial insect sprays and traps, has no odour and is kind to the environment.
Denise Richardson, Goulburn, NSW.

- To help keep your washing-up gloves tidy, peg them onto a hook under the kitchen sink cupboard. They won't stick together and will be dry when you need them.
Rana Robertson, Indented Head, Vic.

- To remove the skin from roasted nuts, place them in a clean cloth or tea towel and rub hard for a minute. The husks will fall off easily.
Lou Nelson, Bourke, NSW.

- To help preserve cucumbers, try slicing them into a container. Cover them with a solution of vinegar, sprinkle of sugar and a few mint leaves.
R. Prior, Salisbury North, SA.

- When baking croutons or quiche cases out of bread, try saving the crusts as they are great with dips.
Felicity Lello, Henley Beach South, SA.

- To defrost your freezer, sprinkle sugar on the ice and carefully remove it with a rubber spatula. That way you'll ensure you don't damage the coils.
Rhonda Stratis, Revesby, NSW.

- Run a vegetable peeler along the edge of a block of chocolate to create quick decorative curls for desserts and cakes.
A. Guthridge, Mount Gambier, SA.

- If you have an abundance of fresh herbs or garlic, chop them up and mix with softened butter. Roll into a log shape, wrap in baking paper and freeze. Cut off a slice as you need it.
Michaela Yannis, Perth, WA.

- To stop eggs sticking to the pan, first line the pan with baking paper. This makes it easy to clean the pan, too.
  Anne Kelly, Queanbeyan, NSW.

- If a cake recipe calls for two eggs, simply use one and substitute a tablespoon of vinegar for the second egg.
  Natalie Moore, Darwin, NT.

- Try stacking paper plates in between your fine china to prevent any damage.
  Maureen Buckley, Noble Park, Vic.

- Store your leftover tomato paste in ice-cube trays, label it and freeze to use later.
  Marilyn Tants, Cranbourne, Vic.

- To keep spring onions fresh and crisp, wrap them in foil and they'll last two weeks or longer. Chop up the green tops and freeze for stews and casseroles.
  Rebecca Burns, Mollymook, NSW.

- Instead of spraying insecticide in your pantry to get rid of moths, just keep an open packet of Epsom salts on a shelf.
  Graham Harwood, Elizabeth, SA.

WACKY BUT IT WORKS

After gardening, clean your hands by rubbing a little sugar and olive oil between your palms. It will remove the grime and soften your skin.
Lucinda Ward, Ipswich, Qld.

KITCHEN/COOKING

21

- To keep a large block of cheese fresh for as long as possible, wrap it in aluminium foil after opening.
Mica Heibel, Mt Gambier, SA.

- Be vigilant about sharpening your cooking knives as this can save you precious hours when prepping your vegetables.
Natalie Doyne, Boisdale, Vic.

- Use toothpicks to keep cling wrap from smudging cream or icing on desserts. Stick a few on the top and sides to holds the wrap above the cream. The toothpick holes are easily smoothed over when serving the dessert.
Alana Everard, Clarinda, Vic.

- Keep root ginger in the freezer and it will last longer than in the fridge.
John Lucas, Moorebank, NSW.

- Only fold biscuit dough two or three times. Any more will result in heavy biscuits.
Miriam Crane, Mount Richmond, Vic.

- When cooking mushrooms, a dash of soy sauce will improve the flavour enormously.
Deanna Singleton, Chipping Norton, NSW.

KITCHEN/COOKING

- For the best shortcrust pastry, remove it half-cooked from the oven, brush with egg white, sprinkle with caster sugar, then return to the oven to finish cooking.
Lisa Jordan, Menai, NSW.

- Soggy tomato sandwiches will be a thing of the past if you cut the tomatoes downwards instead of across. The slices stay much firmer.
Angelica Hale, Newcastle, NSW.

- Use a medicine glass instead of measuring spoons – it's more accurate and causes less spills.
Sally Brock, Geelong, Vic.

- If you buy a steamer set, you can cook lots of vegies at one time, using only one hot plate. It's great when entertaining.
Carol Messenger, Red Cliffs, Vic.

Scrambled eggs with go further if a tablespoon of evaporated milk is added for every two eggs.
Ann Miles, Port Macquarie, NSW.

- Don't panic if your custard curdles. Just remove it from the heat at once and tip it into a bowl. Add a little cold water and whisk vigorously.
Joanne Dawson, Lithgow, NSW.

KITCHEN/COOKING

● When reheating pasta in the microwave, make a small empty circle in the middle of your plate so the pasta will cook evenly and will save you stirring it several times.
Erika Chandler, Orange, NSW.

● Remember that warm water freezes much quicker than cold water the next time you need ice cubes in a hurry.
Winifred Moss, Bathurst, NSW.

● Keep lettuce crisp for weeks by wrapping it completely in paper towel and placing in a freezer bag. Close to keep the air out and store in the crisper compartment of the fridge.
Elisa Lewis, Grafton, NSW.

● Make your own stock cubes with gravy left over from a roast. Just pour the gravy into an ice-cube tray and freeze until needed.
Rosa Barker Devonport, Tas.

● If your honey crystallises, take the lid off the jar and microwave on high for 45 seconds or until the crystals dissolve. Or, stand the open jar in a pan of hot water.
Angie Mullins, Albany, WA.

- Give stewed apples a delicious toffee taste. Sweeten using soft brown sugar instead of white.
Felicia Wood, Warrnambool, Vic.

- If, like me, you find using oven mitts cumbersome in the kitchen, use thick gardening gloves instead. You'll find gripping hot pots and other utensils so much easier, and you won't burn yourself.
Dave Nicholson, Yanchep, WA.

- Make your own chocolate by combining melted chocolate buttons, vanilla essence, sultanas and almonds and let it set in a chocolate box mould. Not only is it inexpensive, you can also make your favourite combinations.
Freda Patrick, Walmul, Qld.

- To avoid sticky fingers while chopping dried fruit for cooking, place it in the fridge for an hour then cut with a warm knife.
Melinda Lane, Suffolk Park, NSW.

- A quick and easy way to get rid of any lingering smells in the kitchen is to bake orange peel in the oven. The citrus smell will leave your kitchen smelling lovely.
Dixie Bell, Collie Cardiff, WA.

WACKY BUT IT WORKS

Always clean from the top down. That way, if any dust escapes your cloth, it'll just land on the floor which you're about to vacuum anyway.
Brittany Bradley, Penrith, NSW.

KITCHEN/COOKING

🔵 When you have boiled eggs, a great way to be able to easily recognise them from fresh eggs is to draw faces on them before storing them.
Sherry Anderson, Port Arthur, Tas.

🔴 When having to take cakes for the school fete, I use a cut down cereal packet for a tray. The top side of the box can be used to line the bottom and adds extra strength. Pop in the cakes and cover with cling wrap – no more lost dishes.
Julie Stevens, Eaton, WA.

🔵 Adding garlic at different stages in your cooking will create different intensities. When you add it immediately to a recipe, you will have a subtle taste, while adding it towards the end will give you a burst of flavour.
Lynette Bailey, Lake Conjola, NSW.

🔴 To keep a cake from drying out and going stale, place half an apple inside the cake tin with it. A lemon will also work just as well.
Lila Rose, Melbourne, Vic.

To make spreading your butter on toast easier, place it between two slices so that it melts from the combined heat. It will become soft and much easier to spread!
Edwin Massey, Calliope, Qld.

- When you're cooking pasta, to prevent the water from boiling over, after you put the water on the stove to heat up, add a dollop of oil to the pot. The oil in the water keeps everything under control when you later add the pasta to cook.
Velma Gonzales, Northampton, WA.

- A capsicum with three bumps on the bottom is sweeter than one with four, while one with four bumps will tend to be a crunchier firmer capsicum. So before purchasing your next capsicum determine what's more important to you – crunchiness or sweetness?
Nadine Morales, Wembley Downs, WA.

- Don't pack your freezer too tightly – it will stop the air from circulating properly.
Pamela Luna, Maroubra, NSW.

- To avoid soft fruit and vegies from bruising, line the fridge crisper with bubble wrap. It's a great way to prolong the life of your produce.
Anna King, Parafield Gardens, SA.

KITCHEN/COOKING

27

- When cooking green vegetables, add a pinch of bicarb of soda to keep the colour vibrant.
  Jacky Kraft, Middleton, SA.

- To stop your Teflon-coated pans from scratching when storing them, place non-stick mats in the bottom of each pan before stacking.
  Jean Lynch, Rockingham, WA.

- Always use tongs to turn meat on the barbecue as using a fork pierces the sealed surfaces and releases the juices, making the meat dry out.
  Freda McCarthy, Young, NSW.

- Put your spice bottles in a basket and label the lids with sticky dots labels.
  L. Ryan, Bilinga, Qld.

- To protect your cookbooks from any spills while cooking, cover the pages with plastic cling wrap – it keeps them looking as good as new.
Abraham Peters, Brisbane, Qld.

- For those who want just a touch of the flavour of garlic or ginger in their cooking, pierce the pieces with toothpicks so you can easily remove them.
Robin Cross, Surrey Downs, SA.

- To save leftover melted chocolate, pour it onto some foil and spread as thin as you can. Let it set in the fridge and then break it up to use as decoration for cakes and desserts.
Sue Frazer, Bateau Bay, NSW.

WACKY BUT IT WORKS

My kids love having a cool bubble bath on a hot day in their blow up paddling pool. They love the novelty of bathing outside and they can splash around without drenching the bathroom.
Susan Scali, Kirwan, Qld

KITCHEN/COOKING

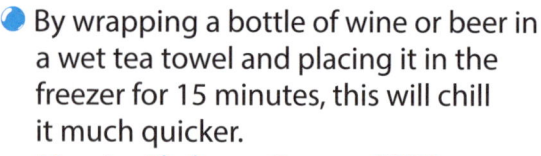

- By wrapping a bottle of wine or beer in a wet tea towel and placing it in the freezer for 15 minutes, this will chill it much quicker.
Maurice Shelman, Orange, NSW.

- When lining a tin with baking paper, use clothes pegs to keep it in place. This stops the paper from curling up and makes the tin easier to fill with mixture. Remove the pegs before baking.
Virginia Harper, St Agnes, SA.

- To gain more bench space in your kitchen, buy a chopping board that fits over your sink. It'll also hide dirty dishes if unexpected guests drop by.
Andres Burns, Tallebudgera, Qld.

- Create homemade peppermint tea by placing a handful of fresh mint leaves into a teapot of boiling water. Allow to sit for five minutes and enjoy.
Jessica Blake, Melba, ACT.

A syringe filled with icing makes an excellent cake decorating tool.
Cheryl Pruss, Glenmore Park, NSW.

- Cook bacon quickly in a sandwich press. It will cook both sides in a few minutes.
Daniel Black, City Beach, WA.

- Make chocolate covered strawberries by filling an ice-cube tray with melted chocolate, place strawberries in and freeze.
Janette Newman, Port Douglas, Qld.

- If you're out of buttermilk, simply mix one cup of milk with one tablespoon of lemon juice – it will do the trick.
Julia Davis, Casuarina, NT.

- Wrap the top of your banana bunch in plastic wrap to make them last up to five days longer.
Chloe Jenkins, Hobart, Tas.

- If you're unsure whether your eggs are hard-boiled or not, spin them on your bench! Hard-boiled eggs spin easily, while raw eggs won't.
Lillian Cameron, Samford, Qld.

KITCHEN/COOKING

- Keep a small magnifying glass in the kitchen to help read the tiny print on food packages.
Kim Wilson, Onkaparinga, SA.

- When cutting vegetables and meat into small portions, use a pizza cutter to make the job a lot quicker and easier.
Liz Bradley, Rosebud West, Vic.

- I love lazy Susans so much that I installed a couple in my fridge. Now I can reach the ingredients at the back without having to pull everything out.
Edith Spielvogel, Mount Albert, Vic.

- Protect your pots and pans, especially the non-stick ones, from scratches by placing each one in an old pillowcase when you store them.
Debbie Lewis, Willow Vale, Qld.

- To remove shells from boiled eggs, simply drain off the hot water once the eggs are cooked then firmly holding the saucepan lid, shake the saucepan vigorously for a short time. Next, add cold water so the eggs can be handled easily. The shells will just peel away.
Trina Parker, Alexandria, NSW.

KATHLEEN TRIES IT OUT!

WACKY BUT IT WORKS

When buttering your crackers, place them on a slice of bread first. When you press down, the bread will stop the cracker from breaking, keeping it in perfect shape for the next ingredient.

- Want to keep the fizz in a bottle of lemonade once opened? Simply drop a raisin into the bottle.
Leonie Griffiths, Gymea, NSW.

- When preparing sandwiches for school or work, place plastic wrap on the bench first. Any crumbs or mess will wrap up with the finished sandwich, leaving your bench clean.
Cecile Rosewarne, Albury, NSW.

- I decluttered my cupboards by installing hooks on the roof of my shelves then hanging my mugs from them. This leaves more shelf space for plates and bowls.
Elinor Stenhouse, Wellington, NZ.

- To revive limp carrots and celery, place in a bowl of water and store in the fridge for two hours.
Beth Wingate, Mount Gravatt, Qld.

KITCHEN/COOKING

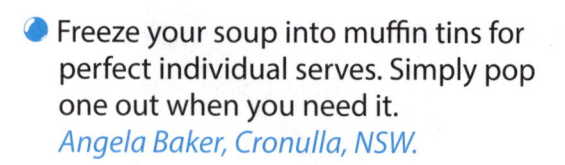

- Freeze your soup into muffin tins for perfect individual serves. Simply pop one out when you need it.
Angela Baker, Cronulla, NSW.

- You can save your tomato sauce for up to three months by simply freezing it. When you need some, cut a slice off with a sharp knife and allow to thaw.
Jemima Beaven, Southbank, Vic.

- To stop cheese from going mouldy, try slipping a couple of sugar cubes into your cheese packet in the fridge.
Brenda Scully, Kingston Beach, Tas.

Squeeze lemon juice over leftover avocado and wrap in cling wrap. This will stop it from turning black.
Russell Haines, Herveys Range, Qld.

- Place potatoes into cold, salted water for about 15 minutes before baking. They will cook in half the time.
Carol Mitchell, Manjimup, WA.

- For easy-to-eat slices of kiwifruit, simply peel skin with a potato peeler and slice with an egg slicer.
Pauline Gooding, Woomelang, Vic.

- For instant icing, pop a giant chocolate button on top of your muffins as they come out of the oven.
Sofia Mavis, St Kilda, Vic.

- I can never remember the conversions for measurements and my recipes always seem to measure in gallons instead of cups. Now I keep a cheat sheet pinned inside my pantry so I don't need to look up the answer.
Rosalie Skipper, Brisbane, Qld.

KITCHEN/COOKING

🔴 Use kebab skewers to cook multiple sausages on the barbecue. By skewering them together, you can turn them over all at once.
Gina Dichiera, Landsdale, WA.

🔵 When making mint sauce, dip the mint leaves in vinegar before chopping them and they'll retain their bright green colour.
Marie Matheson, Emu Plains, NSW.

🔴 When using sundried tomatoes, keep the oil in which they're stored. It has an amazing flavour and can be used in salad dressings, stir-fries and pizza sauces.
Helen Tranter, Bargo, NSW.

🔵 To make grating cheese easier, use a vegetable peeler. It produces a longer, thinner slice of cheese that doesn't clump together. It also helps to make the cheese go further – great for the waistline and the wallet.
K. Patrick, North Bundaberg, Qld.

🔴 If you've forgotten to take the butter out of the refrigerator for making pastry, don't bother to soften it. Just grate it coarsely onto a plate to use.
F. Rooney, Sale, Vic.

- Use toothpicks to cut even slices of cake. Place the cake on a flat surface then stick the toothpicks halfway up the sides, 7cm apart. Rest the blade edge of a long serrated knife across each toothpick, then gently cut the cake.
R. Owen, Helensvale, Qld.

- To keep sandwiches that aren't going to be eaten right away fresh, cover them with lettuce leaves and a clean tea towel – they'll stay fresh without drying out.
Gerard Hines, Manly, Qld.

- When you separate eggs, always beat the egg whites first, before the yolks, as clean beaters offer the best result for egg whites.
Phyllis Sio, Southbank, Vic.

WACKY BUT IT WORKS

Keep a card with all your details on it in your wallet in a visible place. If anything happens to you while you're out and about, someone may save your life.
Patrick Galvin, Moree, NSW.

KITCHEN/COOKING

37

LAUNDRY

38

LAUNDRY

LAUNDRY

- Dry clothes in the sun whenever you can and, on cold on wet days, put your clotheshorse over the bath or in a warm spot in the house to save money.
Kiara Leighton, Noosa, Qld.

- Keep your laundry fresh by making sure you clean the dryer's filters. The moisture from wet clothes can get trapped in the lint attracting mould and bacteria.
Marissa Connor, Ingleburn, NSW.

- Put a layer of aluminium foil underneath your ironing board cover. You can iron at a lower temperature and still get perfect, crease-free results.
Wanda Buchanan, Geelong, Vic.

KATHLEEN TRIES IT OUT!

WACKY BUT IT WORKS

New shoes always slip on the floor! To save embarrassment, Carry a potato in your bag, snap a bit off and rub it on the soles of your shoes every few hours. The starch in the spud will stop you slipping. Magic!

- If you accidentally leave clothes in the washing machine and they begin to smell, put a capful of fabric softener in the dispenser and put the load on prewash cycle. It's quick and you'll have clean sweet-smelling clothes in no time.
Lorenzo West, Chippendale, NSW.

- You can whiten yellowed socks by putting them in a wash bag with a few strips of lemon peel and tossing them in the washing machine.
Josephine Bush, Sandy Bay, Tas.

- Lightly starching pillowcases will help prevent cosmetics from staining them.
Marion Best, Newtown, NSW.

- Use a sheet of baking paper when ironing to protect delicate materials and to prevent the iron from sticking to T-shirt logos.
Jennifer Mullins, Moss Vale, NSW.

- If you want to dry something quickly, pop it in the dryer with a dry towel. It will help speed up the drying time and will save you money on electricity, too.
Theresa Holmes, Castle Hill, NSW.

LAUNDRY

- By tumble drying your pillows once a week for 15 minutes, this will refresh them and get rid of dust mites.
  Lola Torres, Gunbar South, NSW.

- Unshrink clothes by soaking the shrunken piece of clothing in lukewarm water and baby shampoo, work through to relax the fibres, and gently stretch.
  Carolyn Meyer, Kellyville, NSW.

- Spray a man's handkerchief with fabric softener and place in the dryer with your wet clothes. This removes the static, especially from underwear.
  Glenda Vamos, Dandenong, Vic.

- Add one cup of white vinegar to the wash cycle when laundering dark clothes – it helps prevent fading.
  Viv Lomas, Tuggerah, NSW.

- Add two capfuls of eucalyptus oil to your wash – it's wonderful for getting stubborn stains and odours out of sportswear, overalls, towels and sheets.
Mavis Dobson, Gosnells, WA.

- To brighten white shirts add 100ml white vinegar to the wash cycle. The vinegar won't discolour logos.
N. Mitchell, Peakhurst, NSW.

- To keep trousers crease-free, cut a slit in a tube of cardboard and slip it onto a coat hanger. The rounded shape helps prevent crease lines where the trousers hang.
Mary Maucher, Orelia, WA.

- Sew down pockets that are never used to cut down ironing time.
Von Paltridge, Narre Warren South, Vic.

- To clean your washing machine, fill it with warm water and a pint of vinegar.
Riley Cox, Northwood, SA.

- To create more room to dry washing, attach a broom handle (or timber beam) to an old car roof-rack and hang it on your garage wall.
Wendy Wallin, Deception Bay, Qld.

- I've stapled a plastic envelope to my laundry cabinet to hold a laundry and household stain removal guide and any washing instruction labels from recently bought clothes. Now, it's always easy to find exactly what I need.
Hugh Sharp, Cockburn, WA.

LAUNDRY

43

- A tablespoon of white vinegar in the final rinse is an effective natural fabric softener.
Clarissa Smith, Mt Isa, Qld.

- To make use of ceiling space in your laundry, install a coat rail to hang shirts to dry.
Sharni Spence, Avoca Beach, NSW.

- If you're having trouble keeping your coat hangers on the line in windy weather, cut strips from old rubber gloves, loop these over the line and hang hangers from these. The shirts will dry in no time and won't fly off to the neighbour's house.
Loretta Clark, Ballajura, WA.

- Before you toss out your empty shampoo or fabric softener bottle, simply uncap and pop it into your laundry hamper/basket. The bottle still holds a nice scent and it will leave your laundry basket with a slightly more pleasant smell than before.
Angela Sikiric, Cronulla, NSW.

- When your washing machine starts to smell, hang an air freshener inside. Just remember to remove it in between washes.
Susan Reed, Zetland, NSW.

- To stop brand new red-dyed clothes from bleeding over your other laundry, soak it in vinegar before its first wash cycle.
Christina Hatzis, Yokine, WA.

- When washing a woollen underlay in your washing machine, first place it inside a quilt cover. The fluff can easily be shaken out of the cover when finished.
Marjorie Smith, Bli Bli, Qld.

- Rather than pay for professional cleaning, you can safely clean many down-filled items yourself using a low-sudsing, mild detergent. When machine washing, a large front-loading washer is best.
Sam Nyugen, Parramatta, NSW.

WACKY BUT IT WORKS

No lint roller? No worries! Simply dab sticky tape onto your clothes to remove everything from dust to pet hair. When you're done, just throw the tape in the bin.
Jan Kent, Mackay, Qld.

To keep spiders out of your washing, every couple of months squirt surface spray in the holes of your clothesline where they hide, to keep them under control.
Marilyn Tants, Cranbourne, Vic.

LAUNDRY

45

- Use shampoo to wash your woollens instead of wool wash. They'll be just as soft.
Jean Harris, Gladstone, Vic.

Adding eucalyptus oil to a clothing wash gives a beautiful smell and freshness to the clothes, while also lowering the risk of moths and silverfish!
Annette Harding, Bondi Junction, NSW.

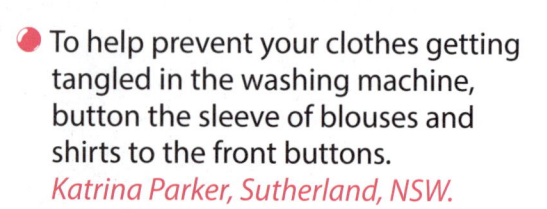

- To help prevent your clothes getting tangled in the washing machine, button the sleeve of blouses and shirts to the front buttons.
Katrina Parker, Sutherland, NSW.

- If you want your linen to be snowy white, just add a few teaspoons of bicarbonate of soda to the washing powder when you wash them.
N. Kane, St Kilda, Vic.

- When drying your shirts and tops, peg them on the clothesline by the underarms. This will prevent noticeable peg marks.
Paul Basquez, Rosebery, Tas.

- If you're hand-washing baby knitwear or other small delicate items, use a salad spinner to remove excess water before drying.
Teri Boyd, via email.

- When you have to use your tumble dryer in winter, move it into your living room and it will dry your clothes and heat up the room at the same time, saving money on heating.
Lorraine Barnes, Lismore, NSW.

- If you don't have a clothes brush, dampen a face washer or the end of a towel and use this to wipe the lint from clothing. It works just a well and costs nothing.
Clifford Bennett, Huntfield Heights, SA.

- To avoid losing socks in the washing machine, secure the pair together with a pin before putting them in. You'll never have odd socks again!
Carol Pratt, Craigieburn, Vic.

WACKY BUT IT WORKS

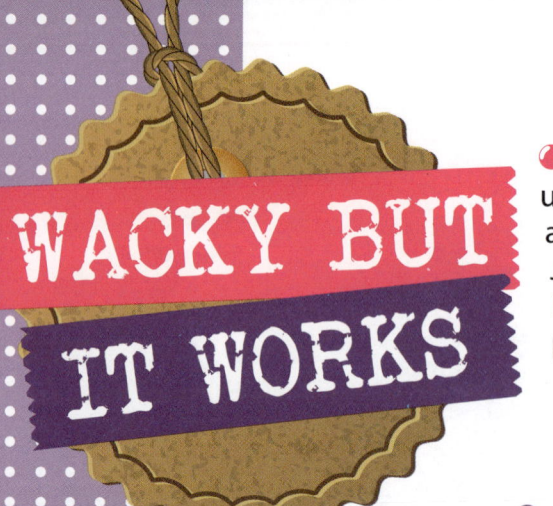

- If your pant hem comes undone when you're out and about, don't panic! Just use a paper clip to hold the loose hem in place until you're able to sew it up properly.
Ann-Marie Prendergast, Noosa, Qld.

- Sick of the dizzying cleaning toxins? Try cleaning your toilet with Gatorade instead! Simply pour two cups of the drink into the toilet and allow to sit for one hour. Wipe down the inside before flushing and it will be sparkling new.
Wilma Peters, Tamworth, NSW.

- Stick something small but easily noticeable like a paper clip at the end of your sticky tape roll. You won't be searching for the end anymore.
Olga Wilson, Griffith, ACT.

- Remove lipstick stains from your clothing by rolling a piece of white bread into a ball and then blotting the lipstick mark. After the stain has been lifted, pop it into the washing machine as usual.
Maryanne Cowper, Albany, WA.

- Hairspray can be used on so much more than just hair. It helps when you have a skirt or dress that keeps riding up when you walk and is also fantastic to use if you have a straw hat that needs a bit of brightening up.
Rose Ellis, Dubbo, NSW.

- I made boiled eggs for breakfast recently, but realised I had no egg cups to eat them out of. Thankfully, hubby had just thrown out his old deodorant can and I used the lid. It worked perfectly.
F. Harrison, Devonport, Tas.

- My husband's buttons are always popping off his pants. So I decided to sew them on with fishing wire and now they stay put.
Cathy Garcia, Newstead, Qld.

- A tennis racquet makes an ideal emergency strainer in the kitchen.
Gita Hogg, Charters Towers, Qld.

- Vegemite is a wonderful healer for cold sores. Dab onto the affected area and you should notice a difference the next day.
Dorothy Doyle, Greensborough, Vic.

- I always keep a sandwich bag by the phone so that if it rings when my hands are dirty, I can still pick it up instantly.
Penny Jones, Charters Towers, SA.

KATHLEEN TRIES IT OUT!

WACKY BUT IT WORKS

STAIN REMOVAL

STAIN REMOVAL

STAIN REMOVAL

- If you spill red wine on the carpet or your clothing, immediately pour some soda water onto the stain, then clean it off. The bubbles help remove the stain.
Claudine Wengret, Parramatta, NSW.

- A rubber eraser dipped in emery powder (available at most hardware stores) is great for cleaning rusted or corroded metal.
Daniel Wells, Schofields, NSW.

- To remove tea and coffee stains, put some salt in a wet cup and rub your fingers back and forth around the cup to remove stains before washing as normal.
Ita Neville, Osborne Park, WA.

- To remove a white heat ring from a wooden table, place a folded, light-coloured towel over the mark and iron it with a steam iron. Make sure you keep the iron moving at all times.
Erin Khalid, Milperra, NSW.

- To remove permanent marker from lunch boxes, go over the writing with a whiteboard marker and then wipe off.
Deanne Frosini, Wyoming, NSW.

- To remove biro marks from vinyl furnishing, simply cut an apple in half and rub briskly over the biro mark until it is gone, then wipe over with a clean damp cloth.
Ness Halliday, Forster, NSW.

- Use toothpaste to clean stained crockery. It's safe, cheap and you always have it in the house.
Sally Holmes, Broome, WA.

- To get blood out of fabrics, use hydrogen peroxide. Apply it directly to the stain and then launder in the washing machine.
Tania Young, Mt Isa, Qld.

- WD40 will remove crayon from almost all hard surfaces, including television screens.
John Stevens, Exmouth, WA.

- An easy way to remove chewing gum from clothing, upholstery or carpets is to heat some white vinegar in a pan and apply it to the gum.
Cassandra Erickson, Greystanes, NSW.

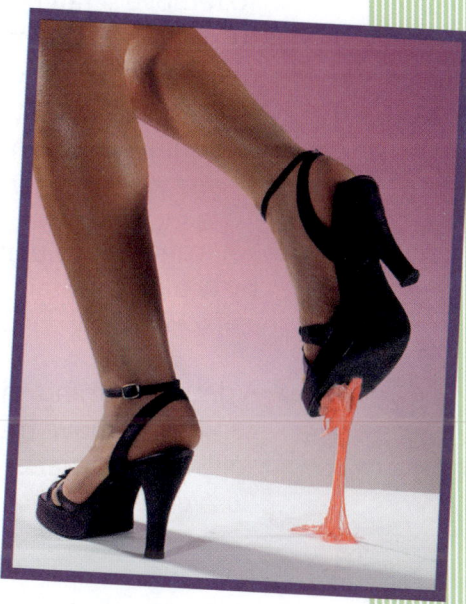

STAIN REMOVAL

53

- To clean oil-based paint off of your hands, use vegetable oil, then wash hands with warm soapy water.
Teresa Schinaia, Hammondville, NSW.

- To remove beetroot stains from clothing or tablecloths, try soaking the item in milk for several hours, then wash as normal.
Elle Parkes, Mackay, Qld.

Remove carrot and pumpkin stains left on cooking utensils, especially chopping boards and food processor parts, by wiping them with a paper towel dabbed in vegetable oil.
Tori Sweetin, Lorne, Vic.

- Tea-tree oil will effectively get rid of fungus. Add ½ teaspoon to a bucket of hot water and sponge on to bathroom tiles.
Danielle Lucas, Port Adelaide, SA.

- To remove scratches from wood furniture, rub with petroleum jelly. This causes the marks to blend in with the wood colour, which also makes the surface look nice and shiny and unmarked.
Denise Vincenzo, Bundaberg, Qld.

- You can remove pen stains from clothes by wiping the stain with hand sanitiser.
Holly Hennessy, Jaloran, WA.

- A dab of foaming shaving cream can help remove many red wine spills from carpets.
Carole Parks, Fairymeadow, NSW.

STAIN REMOVAL

- Hairspray will help to remove marker pen off hard surfaces. Simply spray on the affected area and then wipe it off.
Jean Webster, Darlington, NSW.

- To remove those annoying fingerprints from stainless-steel appliances, place a small amount of baby oil on a napkin and wipe over the affected areas. The fingerprints will just wipe away.
Jaime Ortiz, via email.

- If you have deodorant stains on your clothes, gently sponge the area with white vinegar. Leave for a few minutes before washing in hot water.
Doreen May, Brandy Creek, Vic.

- An easy way to remove mildew stains is to mix salt and lemon juice and wipe over the stain. It works like a charm!
Felicia Powell, Jindabyne, NSW.

WACKY BUT IT WORKS

Grab a rag and baby oil and put away the chemical sprays. A quick scrub with baby oil cuts away kitchen grime and is a great way to buff metal appliances.
Lena Pappas, Kiama, NSW.

STAIN REMOVAL

55

- To remove lipstick stains from your clothes, dab the area with a few drops of eucalyptus oil, leave for 10 minutes and then wash as usual. The stain will vanish in the machine.
Amanda Ratherford, Woy Woy, NSW.

- Get rid of tomato stains from clothes by soaking the garment in one tablespoon of vinegar and then washing as normal.
Ruth Thompson, Hobart, Tas.

- Place a damp cloth over a carpet stain, and press it with an iron set to high. The steam will release the stain.
Fay Hopkins, Birrong, NSW.

- To remove highlighter stains from school clothes, saturate the garment in salted water then put it in a plastic bag and place it in the freezer overnight. Launder as usual the next day.
Danielle Noll, Bargo, NSW.

🟢 Rub a little dishwashing liquid into oily stains on clothing before washing. The stains will disappear.
Jenny Whitford, Port Macquarie, NSW.

- 🟢 To rid rust from the chrome work on your car, rub it with dampened crumpled aluminium foil. It really works!
  M. T. Matheson, Emu Plains, NSW.

- 🟢 To remove car grease from clothes, blot the stain with acetone-based nail polish remover on a paper towel.
  Ron Jones, Katherine, NT.

- 🟢 Use clear make-up remover to remove cosmetic stains from fabrics, then wash in the machine.
  Jayde Taylor, Mordialloc, Vic.

- 🟢 Deal with carpet stains with a couple of drops of dishwashing detergent applied directly and wiped over with a wet sponge.
  Lurline Parsons, Milperra, NSW.

- 🟢 Scrub stained pavers with a mixture of fabric stain remover and water to spruce them up.
  Anna Duricek, Greystanes, NSW.

STAIN REMOVAL

- A quick way to prevent car duco from rusting is to paint the chips and holes with a similar-coloured (or clear) nail varnish. Remember to clean the surface first.
B. Urban, Tewantin, Qld.

- If you are out to dinner at a restaurant, or even if grease splatters on you while you are cooking, use artificial sweetener immediately to blot the stain. The fine powder will absorb the oil.
Fiona Jenkins, Dapto, NSW.

- To remove ink stains from coloured clothes, a milk bath will often do the trick. Just soak the affected garment in milk overnight and launder as usual the next day.
Adrienne Parker, Ashfield, NSW.

- If your toddler just went wild with a ballpoint pen on your new white shirt. Squirt the stain with hairspray and the marks should come right off.
Tamika Solus, Moorebank, NSW.

- Got a ring around your shirt collar from sweat? Cheap hair shampoo will break down body oils and act as a detergent.
Ashleigh Wong, Subiaco, WA.

- Take a can of non-gel shaving cream and spray it onto a tomato sauce stain, rub it in gently and let it dry before washing as normal.
Alan Richardson, Hawthorn, Vic.

- If your child grazes their knees and gets blood stains on their school uniform, don't despair! It seems ridiculous, but soaking bloodstains overnight in cola removes them. Try it.
Regina Long, Richmond, Vic.

- To remove stains from a laminated benchtop, dip a cotton wool ball in glycerine and rub lightly.
Virginia Jones, Forster, NSW.

WACKY BUT IT WORKS

You can remove burnt plastic from things like the toaster with nail polish remover.
Alyssa Townsend, Cairns, Vic.

STAIN REMOVAL

59

WACKY BUT IT WORKS

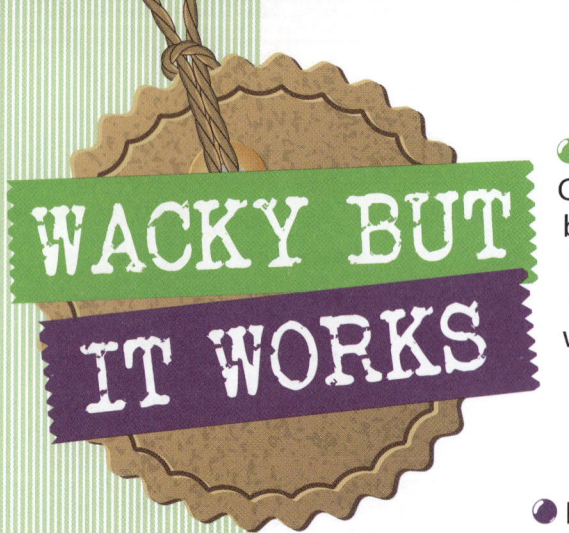

● Need a few more Christmas tree ornaments but don't have the money? Use any star, tree or bell shaped cookie cutters. Just wrap them in ribbon and attach a piece of string.
Anthony Fuentes, Toowoomba, Qld.

● If you need a clutch bag in an emergency, just put your lippie, car keys and tampon into a pitta bread, remembering to hold it the right way up.
Sherry Connick, Sorrento, Vic.

● Wipe a lemon wedge inside your mug to get rid of tea stains, then wash with soapy water. Your cup will be clean as new!
Zoe Lock, Balmoral, NSW.

● Lining your lunch box with bubble wrap is a great way to ensure that your fruit doesn't get bruised while you travel to and from school or work.
June Swift, Belair, SA.

KATHLEEN TRIES IT OUT!

● If you don't have a rolling pin handy then simply use a cold can when rolling out dough. Works a treat.
Isabelle Toms, Penguin, Vic.

CLEANING

CLEANING

● To deodorise carpets, sprinkle bicarbonate of soda over them, leave overnight, then vacuum away in the morning.
Tiffany Callum, Canningvale, WA.

● Put a few drops of tea tree oil on some paper towel and place it in the bottom of the bin each time you empty it and your bin will always smell fresh.
Susie Mcdonald, Figtree, NSW.

● A great way to clean your bath without aggravating a bad back is by using a sponge mop.
Skye Walters, Strathfield, NSW.

● To clean a kettle, cut up a lemon and boil in a three quarters full jug. Let it sit for about 15 minutes, then remove the liquid and reboil with fresh water.
Diane Mehavic, Gold Coast, Qld.

● To bring a shine back to your stainless steel appliance, use a cloth and soda water. It'll leave it streak free.
Gail Steele, Picton, NSW.

- To clean your rangehood vent, put it in the bath, cover with water and sprinkle with laundry powder. Leave for 14-20 minutes and it will be sparkling clean.
Leslie Wolfe, Prospect, SA.

- To clean dirty oven racks, place in the laundry tub and cover with hot water, add two dishwashing tablets and leave overnight. Then use a kitchen scourer to scrub off any remaining grime.
Merle Dunn, Golden Grove, SA.

- To keep your fridge door clean from dust and grime, spray lightly with furniture polish.
Kendra Keller, Bundaberg, Qld.

- To get rid of nasty odours in your bin, soak a slice of bread in white vinegar and leave in the bin overnight. The bread will absorb the bad smells.
Christina Walters, Broome, WA.

- To deodorise the inside of your rubber gloves between wash-ups, add a few drops of tea tree oil or oil of clove to bicarbonate of soda and store in a jar. Sprinkle into gloves after each use and shake out excess.
Samuel Arnold, Wollongong, NSW.

WACKY BUT IT WORKS

When eating pasta, I don't like the spaghetti dangling down my chin – the sauce ends up all over my face and clothes! To avoid this, I use scissors to cut up my spaghetti after it's cooked.
Mary Hemmings, Chelmer, Qld.

CLEANING

65

● To remove strong odours from a chopping board, spray with vinegar and leave to dry overnight.
Gwendolyn Arnold, Mawson Lakes, SA.

● Remove stickers from wood surfaces by brushing with white vinegar. Give it time to soak in then gently scrape off.
Denise Clair, Perth, WA.

● If you have a badly burnt saucepan, put a sliced onion in water and boil. The burnt pieces will float to the top.
Andree Braddy, Flinders View, Qld.

● Tip leftover coffee grinds into your sink and pour boiling water over them. Any smells will disappear.
Trudy Magnus, Maitland, NSW.

To use the awkward space near sink pipes and keep cleaning products tidy, install cheap wire baskets on the inside wall of your cupboard under your sink.
Deilia Hawke, West Footscray, Vic.

● To clean copper and brass pots, squeeze some tomato sauce onto a cloth and rub onto the pots. Rinse and dry well.
Terri Robins, Golden Beach, Qld.

CLEANING

- If your plastic containers or cutting boards have stains from food, simply wash them in soapy water and place them outside in the sun to dry. The sun acts like a bleach and the stains disappear.
Raquel McDonald, Goulburn, NSW.

- To help make the cleaning of your fridge easier, line the shelves on the doors with folded kitchen paper. It'll catch drips and crumbs, making the job easier.
Laraine Barker, via email.

- If you don't want to risk scratching your floorboards with a vacuum cleaner, simply run a damp cloth over the dusty spots to pick up any fluff.
Veronica Hawking, Inglewood, SA.

- To keep your toothbrush clean and soft, keep it in a small glass of alcohol-free mouthwash.
Len Stevenson, Cabramatta, NSW.

- To clean up and remove tarnish on pewter or silverware, soak it in warm water with a few drops of dishwashing soap, then rub it with outer cabbage leaves. Buff it with a soft cotton cloth to make it shine.
D. Holmes, Bentleigh, Vic.

If you're spring cleaning, unhook all the curtains and if you don't have time to wash them, hang them on an outside line in the breeze. Giving them a good shake will also help rid them of the dust build-up.
Tasha Soto, Cabramatta, NSW.

- Put a saucer of baking powder at the back of the wardrobe to absorb unpleasant smells.
Angie Taylor, Bedford Park, SA.

- To prevent blockages, regularly put ½ cup of bicarbonate of soda down the drain, followed by ½ cup of vinegar. This works on shower drains and toilets, too. Flush or rinse after an hour. For tricky build-ups you may need to use a commercial drain product.
Emanuel Collier, Perth, WA.

- Avoid streaks when cleaning glass by using a glass cleaner and paper towel. Remove any remaining marks by rubbing with newspaper.
Irene Pappas, Glenelg, SA.

- If the bottom of your shower curtain starts to get mouldy, soak in a bucket with Napisan, then rinse. If the whole curtain needs a clean, detach and soak overnight in the tub with a scoopful of washing detergent. Rinse, then hang up to dry.
Natasha Floyd, Mandurah, WA.

KATHLEEN TRIES IT OUT!

WACKY BUT IT WORKS

If you're cutting up an apple for the kids' lunch boxes, keep it from going brown by holding it together with a rubber band.

- Don't store anything other than clothes and shoes in your wardrobe. Boxes, books or sports equipment will simply encourage more dust and dirt.
Sandy Ryan, Ipswich, Qld.

- To get your crystal gleaming, rinse in one part vinegar to three parts warm water, and air dry.
Allison Henderson, Trinity Beach, Qld.

- When mopping a polished floor, add some eucalyptus oil to your bucket. It creates a lovely shine on the floor, and your house will smell fresh all day.
Sonia Hardy, Waterloo, NSW.

- To dust and clean carved furniture, apply a little cedar oil with an old shaving brush.
Martin Patterson, Bankstown, NSW.

- Give spent dryer sheets a last hurrah by using them to shine your metal taps. You can even use dryer sheets to dust the surfaces of your home, and because they contain anti-static properties, you might find that doing it helps to lessen future dust build-up.
Irma Knight, Cervantes, WA.

CLEANING

● An easy way to clean the glass in your combustion heater is to dampen a cloth, dip it into the ashes and rub it on the glass. Wipe it off and the glass will be clean with no chemicals needed.
Kristin Briggs, Leura, NSW.

● Use a hair dryer to blow the dust off dried plastic flowers.
Jean Griffin, Katherine, NT.

● To keep slate floors looking their best, wash with hot water and a capful of carwash liquid. It gives a lovely shine and a slight wax coating.
Brandi Hardy, Cranebrook, NSW.

● If you have a CD or DVD that seems too scratched to play, put a little vinegar on a tissue and rub over the disc. The vinegar removes the dust and dirt, and makes the disc easier to read.
Sammy Brooks, Bowen, Qld.

- The easiest way to clean venetian blinds is to soak a pair of gloves in soapy water, put them on and then slide each slat of the blinds, one by one, between your fingers.
*Kerry Phelps,
Tamworth, NSW.*

- A glass table will sparkle if a little lemon juice is rubbed into it. Dry, then buff with paper. If there are any scratches, remove them first with toothpaste rubbed in with a soft cloth.
Pippa Cowell, Port Maquarie, NSW.

- To clean skirting boards without bending over, wear an old sock on one foot while vacuuming and wipe your foot along the skirting board as you go.
Rudy Ferguson, Harrisvale, Qld.

- Use a slice of bread to pick up any tiny glass slivers. Press firmly over the area. Be sure you have collected all pieces of the glass before giving the area the all clear.
Marcia Thompson, Rosevale, Qld.

- To restore toilet bowls back to their shiny best, clean with old, flat Coke or Pepsi. To dissolve limescale, leave the soda overnight to soak.
Cora Daniels, Adelaide, SA.

- The stained grout between wall tiles can be touched up with shoe whitener and a fine paint brush.
Maxine Hall, Maroochydore, Qld.

- Put your bleach in an empty squeeze bottle so you can get it into all those hard to reach places in your shower.
Sandy Ortiz, Panania, NSW.

- To keep rust from forming on your shelves or bath ledge from shaving or air freshener cans, paint clear nail polish on the bottom of the rim of the can.
Kerryn Taylor, Ashgrove, Qld.

- To clean your iron, sprinkle salt on a paper bag and then run the hot iron over it.
Wendy Davies, Old Toongabbie, NSW.

- Before you replace a worn-out brush head on an electric toothbrush, use it to clean the grout around the tiles. The machine does a better job than manually scrubbing ever will.
Celia Gross, Willowbank, Qld.

- To stop your bathroom mirror from fogging, clean with shaving cream and a clean cloth.
Violet Ford, Menai, NSW.

- To prevent ash from flying everywhere when cleaning out a fireplace, use a spray bottle filled with water to cover the ashes with a light mist.
Belinda Cox, Brisbane, Qld.

- To remove stubborn marks from floor tiles, squeeze a little toothpaste onto a green scouring pad and rub gently onto the mark, then rinse with clean water.
Joan Buchanan, Broome, WA.

WACKY BUT IT WORKS

Hosting a kids' party is hard when you're money and time-poor. Instead of baking, I buy arrowroot biscuits and coloured icing and let the kids have fun decorating their treats.
Caitlin Kintore, Canada Bay, NSW.

CLEANING

● Wipe out your Esky with hot water and a few drops of vanilla before storing it – there'll be no nasty odours when you next go to use it.
Monique Pope, Marrickville, NSW.

● Clean floors and furniture with a soft cloth dipped in tea and wrung out, then buff dry.
Dora Markson, Dee Why, NSW.

● Don't throw out your old exfoliating glove, use it to clean the bath and sink.
Paula Tallis, Fremantle, WA.

● To clean the bottom of the iron, sprinkle salt on the ironing board and iron back and forth.
Danielle Gilchrist, Nowra, NSW.

● I store each cleaning product along with a cloth or brush in a zip-lock bag. It keeps my cupboards tidy, and I don't have to decide which is the right cloth for each product.
Louise Mason, Wentworthville, NSW.

- You can clean chrome by applying vinegar, then buffing with a soft cloth.
Len Stevens, Narrabri, NSW.

- To clean a stainless steel sink, put the plug in the sink with two denture-cleaning tablets and half fill with water; leave for several hours or overnight and the next day it should be sparkling. Then use the water to clean the draining area of the sink, too.
Lucinda Pickett, Port Macquarie, NSW.

- When your toothpaste tube is almost finished, don't throw it away. The remnants are excellent for cleaning white sports shoes. Just apply with an old toothbrush and your shoes will come up clean and bright.
Mel Davis, Kiama, NSW.

- Place a cup half-filled with water in the microwave and cook on high for a few minutes. The steam will loosen any food spills, making the microwave easy to clean.
Nicola Levin, Brisbane, Qld.

CLEANING

- Clove oil kills mould spores. Mix three drops in one litre of water and then use to wipe down areas susceptible to mould.
Claire Snell, Port Arthur, Tas.

- Disinfect dishcloths by adding a few drops of eucalyptus oil to a sink full of boiling water and soak them. The oil not only has anti-bacterial properties, it creates a fresh fragrance throughout the kitchen and the sink sparkles.
Kristina Hill, Meandarra, Qld.

- Clean jewellery with a cotton bud dipped in gin or whisky. The alcohol will evaporate leaving jewellery bright and sparkling.
Danielle Richards, Geelong, Vic.

- Sprinkle baking powder on your stainless steel sink and leave for a few minutes. Wash off with a wet cloth.
Pam Vickers, Port Adelaide, SA.

- Once you've cleaned the oven with oven cleaner, take large lemons, cut into thick slices and bake for 10 minutes. This will get rid of the oven cleaner smell.
Louise Reeve, Kingswood, NSW.

- An environmentally friendly furniture polish can be made by mixing one teaspoon of lemon oil with 600ml light olive oil. Apply with a soft cloth. The polish will pick up dust instead of flicking it into the air, so it's very good for those who suffer from allergies and asthma.
Glenn Aguilar, Caringbah, NSW.

- To polish silver, place crumpled aluminium foil in a bowl, add water and two tablespoons of salt. Immerse the silver and leave overnight. Rinse and dry with a soft cloth.
Susan Litchfield, Prestons, NSW.

Net onion bags make effective scrubbers to clean your pots and pans and won't leave scratch marks.
Sam Shaw, Nelson Bay, NSW.

- To rid your kitchen of strong, unpleasant odours, place a whole lemon in a baking tin and cover it entirely with water. Bake on medium for 20 minutes. You will be amazed at the beautiful smell wafting through your kitchen.
Caroline Brown, Peakhurst, NSW.

WACKY BUT IT WORKS

I keep a trumpet in the toilet and blow on it whenever I'm doing a number two to warn my family to give it a few minutes before entering.
Terri Dawlish, Liverpool, NSW.

CLEANING

● Clean the gunk that collects around the cutting wheel of a can opener by running a paper towel through it. After a couple of turns back and forth, it'll be good as new and work better, too.
Angela Clarke, Penrith, NSW.

● To polish stainless steel products, use a half-half mix of methylated spirits and baby oil. Your barbecue will never look better!
Sandra Hinds, Runcorn, Qld.

● A great way to clean your bath and get rid of any dirty marks is to mix washing powder and a small amount of water when cleaning.
Carly Wright, Leura, NSW.

To clean polished tiles, dissolve a dishwashing tablet in two cups of boiling water, then cool. It can be used as both a grout and tile cleaner. It's a great alternative to expensive cleaners and really works.
Cassandra Edwards, Hobart, Tas.

● A great use for old, unmatched socks is to wear them on your hands and dust the house with them. Run your hands along chair rails, benches, and doors until the sock is dusty enough to discard or wash and reuse.
Gwendolyn Wilkins, Mirrool, NSW.

- To clean grubby or mouldy shoes, mix a litre of water with ¼ teaspoon of clove oil. Wipe over and leave to dry.
*J. Lynne,
Berkeley Vale, NSW.*

- Make your car vinyl and dashboard sparkle by using humble floor wax. Just rub it on and polish it off for a fraction of the price.
*Joe Connor,
Hervey Bay, Qld.*

- You can remove dishwasher grime, such as stuck-on food or stains, by wiping the inside of the machine with a damp towel sprinkled with baking soda.
Keira Oxley, Bealiba, Vic.

- To stop bathroom mirrors steaming up, regularly rub a dry bar of soap over the surface and rub in with a clean cloth.
Glenda Drake, Merriworth, Tas.

- To safely sterilise glass containers, place a steel spoon into the jar and slowly fill with boiling water. Allow it to stand for a few minutes, then empty and leave to cool.
Ruben Little, Frankston, Vic.

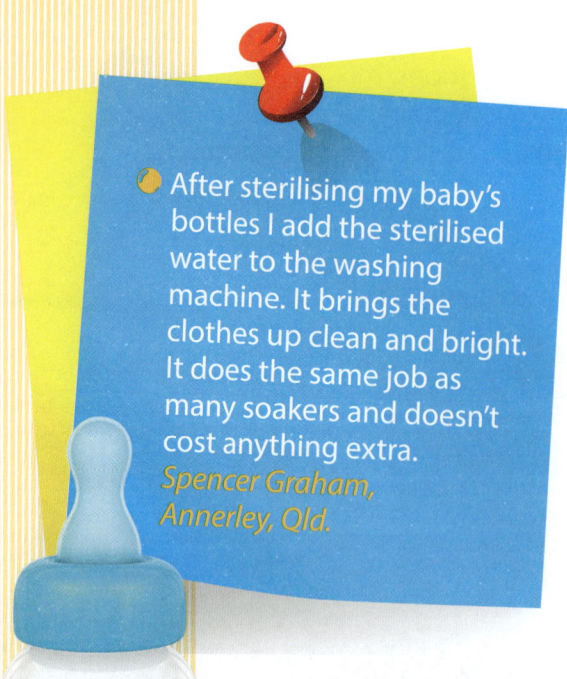

● After sterilising my baby's bottles I add the sterilised water to the washing machine. It brings the clothes up clean and bright. It does the same job as many soakers and doesn't cost anything extra.
Spencer Graham, Annerley, Qld.

● When cleaning your shower, use a watering can to rinse off the cleaning product. This is really helpful when you have a shower head that is fixed to the wall.
Vernia Briner, Auckland, NZ.

● If your plastic storage containers start to smell like the food that was in them, wash them out with hot water and two tablespoons of baking soda.
Jessica Powers, Brunswick, Vic.

● Use your blow-dryer to remove dust from lampshades and delicate curtains.
Rita Clarke, Mitchell Park, SA.

● Place a stocking over your vacuum hose to suction up tiny items, such as earrings and bobby pins.
Trudie Carr, Copacabana, NSW.

● Soak hair brushes and combs overnight in hot water and a good splash of bleach to clean them.
Marilyn Tants, Cranbourne, Vic.

● If you wash you shower curtain with salt water when you first buy it, it will never mould.
Marian Brown, Brucefield, SA.

CLEANING

- To keep shower tiles cleaner for longer, wax them with car polish after giving them a good clean. This will help stop the grime from sticking to them.
Lucy Zimmerman, Melbourne, Vic.

- Use lemon oil to shine bathroom tiles. Lemon oil will also prevent mould and mildew.
Julie Lucas, Bulli, NSW.

- Clean your blender by filling it halfway with warm soapy water. Toss in a handful of ice cubes and run the blender for a minute. This will clean all the crevices and remove the build-up on the blades.
Erika McDean, Kawana North, Qld.

- Clean your ceiling fans by covering the blades with pillowcases and turning the fan on. The dust will fall off into the pillowcase!
Mary Simpson, Ashgrove, Qld.

Don't wipe surfaces in your house that are taller than your tallest friend.
Celia Waterhouse, Alfred Cove, WA.

- An easy way to clean pebbles from your fish tank is to place them in a laundry bag and rinse thoroughly – it's easy and hassle-free.
P. Kidman, Sutherland, NSW.

WACKY BUT IT WORKS

It might sound weird but keep your cling film in the fridge. It is so much easier to use when cold.
Yvette Robinson, Goulburn, NSW.

CLEANING

81

To keep your car clean from muddy football boots, get the kids to put their feet – boots and all – into a plastic bag after a footy match for the journey home.
Amanda Szewczuk, Marion, SA.

- To clean those stubborn cheese bits off your grater, grab an apple, lemon or potato and grate it right after you grate your cheese.
  Erin Toohey, Chipping Norton, NSW.

- If your drain is clogged, pour a cup of salt and a cup of baking soda, followed by a jug full of boiling water, down the drain to clear the blockage.
  M. Wurfel, Hillcrest, SA.

- If you get candle wax on your tiled floor, put a few sheets of paper towel over the top and iron the paper towel with a medium-hot iron. The wax will melt into the towel – problem solved.
  Julie Campbell, Hazelbrook, NSW.

- To clean crayon off your walls, dip a damp cloth in baking soda and wipe the mark off lightly.
  C. Walton, Ferny Hills, Qld.

CLEANING

82

🔵 Baby wipes are useful for quick surface clean-ups in kitchens and bathrooms. They also are great for cleaning up after craft projects.
Sara Osborne, Ballarat, Vic.

🔵 When cleaning timber blinds, use a peg to mark which blade you're up to in case you need to leave in the middle of cleaning.
Julie Jansen, Murrumba Downs, Qld.

🔵 To remove mouldy smells from towels, wash with a teaspoon of bicarbonate of soda. The smell will disappear and will leave your towels lovely and fresh again.
Bridget Mckenzie, Kandanga, Qld.

🔵 Leave a drop of disinfectant or a squeeze of lemon in the bottom of the toilet brush container. This will keep it smelling fresh.
Valerie Sharp, Albany, WA.

🔵 Use shaving foam to get grubby marks off walls.
Annette Arvidson, Sale, Vic.

CLEANING

- For sparkling silver cutlery, fill the sink with warm water and add two teaspoons of laundry soaker. Leave cutlery to soak for an hour. Rinse with warm water and dry with a cloth.
*Deb Brander,
Sunshine Coast, Qld.*

- To clean cobwebs without spreading dust, wet an old sock, pull it over a ruler and wipe over the cobwebs.
Maxine Howard, Tynong, Vic.

- Instead of oven cleaners, try a squeeze of lemon juice to degrease your cooktop.
Wendy Hughes, Newtown, NSW.

- If you find it physically difficult to get down and scrub your shower floor and walls, use a stiff-bristled broom for the job. After scrubbing, rinse with a bucket of warm water containing a couple of drops of lavender oil.
Jane Kelly, Mannum, SA.

- To revive pewter, polish with the outer leaves of a cabbage. Then buff gently with a soft cloth.
Sophia Clements, Ballina, NSW.

- Give kitchen tiles a good clean and then apply furniture polish. Buff to a shine and you'll find that grease will wipe off easily.
Miriam Henderson, Liverpool, NSW.

- When buffing a marble table or benchtop, try using car polish as it leaves a thin, invisible film that helps reduce staining.
Deborah Bowden, Rosebud, Vic.

- A cost-effective way to clean windows is to spray them with white vinegar and wipe clean with newspaper or a paper towel.
Kris Palmer, Singleton, WA.

WACKY BUT IT WORKS

If I ever feel guilty about drinking on my own in the evenings, I go on Facebook and feels like I'm having a glass of wine or two with my friends.
Kristy Simpson, Port Augusta, SA.

- Make your own abrasive cleaner from a mixture of lemon juice and salt. Use to remove stains and mould.
Pat Thornton, Gold Coast, Qld.

- Keep your fridge smelling fresh by placing a box of baking soda on a shelf to absorb bad odours.
Lucy Cousins, Morphett Vale, SA.

- To get rid of scuff marks on a wood floor, cut an 'X' into a tennis ball, slip the ball over a broomstick, and rub the tennis ball back and forth over the scuff marks. They should all disappear.
Patsy Gane, Launceston, Tas.

- When you're using a chamois, rinse it in fabric softener as it will help prevent the cloth from going hard once it has dried.
Traci Snyder, Brighton, Vic.

CLEANING

10 TIPS FOR CLEANING WITH LAVENDER

- Adding one or two drops of lavender oil onto a warm light bulb will immediately infuse your living space with the aroma.
  Ann-Marie Prendergast, Noosa, Qld.

- Place a few drops of lavender oil on the air filter of your vacuum cleaner while vacuuming and your house will smell lovely.
  Sara Lowe, Moana, SA.

- When washing floors, use 15 drops of lavender oil in a full bucket of warm water.
  Wendy Cho, Nakara, NT.

- Put 10 drops of lavender oil onto a towel and place it in your dryer – your clothes will have a lovely, fresh scent.
  Angelina Moretti, Prahran, Vic

- Put five to 10 drops of lavender oil on a cotton ball and place it in your drawer, your gym bag, wardrobe or suitcase, to ward of musty scents.
  Joanna Moore, Alfredton, Vic.

- Add 10 drops of lavender oil to your ironing water – your clothes will smell beautiful.
  Phyllis Hoang, Lismore, NSW.

Place six drops of lavender oil in a spray bottle filled with white vinegar. This is particularly good for cleaning benchtops, bathroom and kitchen basins due to its disinfectant properties.
Ruby Kovac, Buderim, Qld.

- Fill a spray bottle with warm water, add 10-15 drops of lavender essential oil and use it as a natural air freshener.
  Hannah Manthey, Gladstone, Qld.

- Lavender repels insects, so place three to five drops on cotton balls and leave in areas of infestation by insects such as ants, moths and cockroaches. It's even safe enough to put in your pantry.
  Amber Lan, Orange, NSW.

- Make your own lavender dishwashing detergent by adding about 10 drops of oil to a bottle of unscented dish liquid.
  June Swift, Belair, SA.

CLEANING

INDOOR LIVING

INDOOR LIVING

INDOOR LIVING

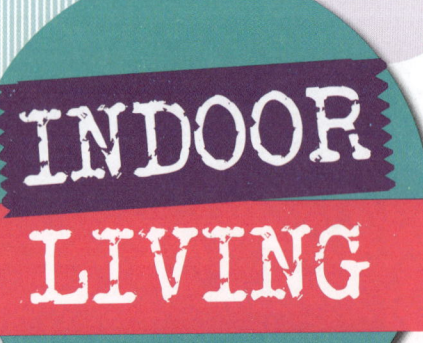

● Wardrobes and cupboards can easily get musty and damp – to help prevent this, spray with a mix of eucalyptus oil and water.
Marion Patterson, Leura, NSW.

● To remove a broken light bulb that's still in its socket, place a thick, dry sponge over the bulb base and turn gently.
Della Holt, Brisbane, Qld.

● The easiest way to keep items tidy in a drawer is to separate them into individual labelled containers. This really does make it easier to find what you're looking for.
Marguerite Mcdonald, Bargo, NSW.

● Place your candles in the freezer for at least two hours prior to burning. It will make them last longer.
Jasmine Pope, Almaden, Qld.

● To make changing a doona easy, put the top corner into the doona cover and secure with a clothes peg on the outside. Then do the same with the other corner and secure with another peg. Pull the cover down over the doona and peg the other two corners. Then shake the doona flat and remove the pegs.
Pearl Brown, Wollongong, NSW.

KATHLEEN TRIES IT OUT!

WACKY BUT IT WORKS

Don't buy expensive air freshener for your bathroom. Instead, place a few drops of essential oil along the inside of your toilet roll. The fragrance lasts for days.

- Use old hanging nappy holders in the bathroom for storage space for small towels and other bathroom items. This leaves plenty of space on the shelves for larger bath towels.
Courtney Moore, Yelarbon, Qld.

- When moving into a new house, consider changing the locks. Some owners and previous tenants might still have copies of the keys.
Christy Hodges, Brighton, Tas.

- If you don't have flyscreens but want to keep the flies out, put a vase of lavender by any open windows – they hate it!
Hattie Palmer, Narromine, NSW.

INDOOR LIVING

- If your flowers are too short for your vase, scrunch up some clear cellophane and place it in the bottom of the vase before adding the blooms and water. It gives the flowers extra height and still looks attractive.
Rhonda Lawson, Tweed Heads, NSW.

- Sprinkle pencil sharpenings on the top of the soil of indoor plants to keep insects at bay.
Maureen Buckley, Noble Park, Vic.

- When you water indoor plants and the water overflows into the tray, remove the water with a cooking syringe. Keep it with your watering can and you'll save a lot of time, wet towels, spills on carpet or stained slate.
L. Kopp, Munster, WA.

- Adding a cup of lemonade to the water in a clear vase of flowers keeps the water clean for weeks and your flowers alive for a lot longer.
Ann-Marie Prendergast, Noosa, Qld.

- Rub floor polish onto light bulbs and then polish to keep the flies and moths away. Castor oil works just as well.
Letitia Wood, Kiama, NSW.

- Store each of your sheet sets inside the matching pillowcase, so they're ready to use and take up less space in the linen press.
Skye Rutherford, Greenacre, NSW.

- To restore finished wood furniture, soak two tea bags in hot water for 10 minutes. Let cool, then dampen a clean soft cloth with tea and wipe over wood furniture. It will bring out the woods natural colour and shine.
Hannah Manthey, Gladstone, Qld.

- To help indoor ferns grow, give them one aspirin tablet diluted in water every month.
Amber Novak, Orange, NSW.

- Instead of folding bath towels, roll them up. You'll be able to store as many towels in the same space.
Willis Park, Cedar Grove, Qld.

- Make a DIY lantern by filling a mason jar with water and adding glow sticks.
Catherine Moss, Macgregor, ACT.

INDOOR LIVING

93

- To rid your house of pesky fruit flies, add lemongrass oil to the water when you mop the floor.
  Donna Thomson, Marrara, NT.

- By replacing your white light bulbs with yellow ones, this will help to not attract as many insects.
  Joanne Parkes, Maroubra, NSW.

- To stop liquid nails and gap filler cartridges from clogging up and drying out when half-used, simply wipe the nozzle clean and seal it with a blob of Blu-Tack – it works like a charm.
  Roy Mckenzie, via email.

- Instead of putting your electric blanket away during summer, leave it on your bed and turn your mattress over. It's a great way to store it, plus you'll be flipping your mattress over every few months like the manufacturers recommend.
  Byron Mcgee, Albion, Qld.

If the seats of your cane furniture are beginning to sag, wash them in warm soapy water and leave to dry in the sun. The cane will shrink back to its original tautness.
Jeannie Byrd, Narooma, NSW.

- Your indoor plants need water, light and warmth to survive. So when you're off on holiday, don't forget about them. Make sure you ask a friend to water them and open the blinds so they get some sun.
  Sophia Nivinson, Fairfield Heights, NSW.

KATHLEEN TRIES IT OUT!

WACKY BUT IT WORKS

🔵 We usually bring our own snacks to the movie, but as a treat we bought a cup of soft drink. They're so expensive, so to get the most money out of our purchase we took the cup home and repurposed it as a custom toothbrush holder.

🔵 Use plastic drinking straws to extend the length of the stems of any flowers in a bunch that are too short for the vase.
Sherry Connick, Sorrento, Vic.

🔵 To make candles last longer, cover with a plastic bag and place in the freezer for 24 hours before lighting.
Stephanie Goodinson, Albany, WA.

INDOOR LIVING

- To locate light switches in the dark, put a dot of luminous paint on tape and stick to the switches.
Will McGowan, Tamworth, NSW.

- To liven up your boring lampshades, sew on some brightly coloured buttons. It updates the lamp and looks really funky and best of all, it costs almost nothing to do.
Phyllis Hoang, Lismore, NSW.

- **To add a bit of humour, hang a corkboard behind your toilet door and pin cut-outs from Take 5, such as funny pets, wise words, kids and jokes. It's priceless to hear your guests and family commenting on them.**
June Swift, Belair, SA.

- If your curtain gapes in the middle when you close them, letting in the light, sew a small magnet into both centre seams at the same height. Your curtains will now close tight.
Ariadne Fox, Katoomba, NSW

- Instead of throwing out old teabags, dry them out in the sun and use them as fire starters for your wood heater.
Angelina Moretti, Prahran, Vic.

- Shoe boxes make thrifty and useful storage containers for DVDs and CDs as they're an ideal size.
Katina Klinakis, Moorooka, Qld.

- If you have a lot of electrical goods in your home, and are unsure which remote goes with which appliance, buy a box of coloured dots and place one on the remote and one on the matching item.
Arabella Gray, Portland, Vic.

- Old unwanted telephone directories make ideal personal address books. Simply cross out the names and addresses of all the people you don't know.
Sara Lowe, Moana, SA.

- If you're putting wallpaper on your walls and having trouble getting into the tight, awkward places, try using a pizza cutter wheel. It works perfectly, especially around light switches.
Harvey Whitford, Sandy Bay, Tas.

- If you suffer from arthritis and find it difficult changing pillowcases, buy a couple of cheap satin pillowcases and keep them on your pillows. When you change your pillowcases they will slip on easily with just a little shake.
Joanna Moore, Alfredton, Vic.

- Print a photo you love on an A4-size piece of paper – be it your favourite holiday destination or your grandkids – laminate it and use it as placemats on your dinner table. They're cheap and make fantastic conversation starters at any dinner party.
Sarah Kennedy, Blacktown, NSW.

- To make it easier to find the right size sheets when changing the beds, mark them in the bottom corners with a permanent marker – S for single, D for double, Q for Queen and K for King.
Coral Harwood, Pacific Pines, Qld.

- Installing dark coloured shades or curtains, and keeping them closed during the hottest portions of the day is going to cool off the room significantly.
Lucy Baker, Narromine, NSW.

- I keep a wet flannel folded in a bag in the freezer. It's handy to use on burns or sprains.
Karen Passmore, Northcote, Vic.

- Once your old towels become too shabby to use, recycle them by cutting them into face washer-size pieces and zig-zag hem them to prevent fraying. Use them as dusters, cloths or even as nappy wipes.
Margaret Ainslie, Sunshine, Vic.

- When lighting lots of candles at once, use a length of raw spaghetti as a taper – it'll stop your fingers getting burned.
Dave Nicholson, Yanchep, WA.

- Instead of using rope or tassles to tie back my curtains, I used a string of beads and a butterfly that I found in a craft shop.
Dale Hawken, Merrylands, NSW.

- I was looking for a way to decorate the brick walls in my new house. I found one of my ornamental fans and fixed it to the wall with Blu-Tack. It's a great conversation piece.
Mary Arena, Coffs Harbour, NSW.

- To make cut flowers last twice as long, put them in a vase of cold tea to which you've added a small amount of bleach.
Yvonne White, Mooloolaba, Qld.

WACKY BUT IT WORKS

You don't want to spend Christmas Day baking if you hate cooking, and you don't have to. Just buy mince pies from the supermarket, heat them up on the day and you can even write the names of your guests on them in icing if you'd like a personal touch.
Wendy Cho, Nakara, NT.

INDOOR LIVING

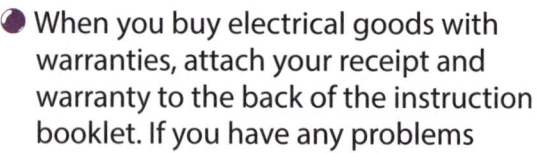

- When you buy electrical goods with warranties, attach your receipt and warranty to the back of the instruction booklet. If you have any problems with the item, it won't be lost.
Priscilla Chan, Norwood, Tas.

- To freshen up a bedside lamp, just add a beaded trim to the bottom rim of the lamp shade. It looks fresh without the cost of a new lamp.
P. Morgan, Port Macquarie, NSW.

- Rather than throwing away old T-shirts, you can turn them into pillows by cutting the sleeves off, stitching up the holes and stuffing with cotton balls.
Eva Battarbee, Yalwal, NSW.

- Are the leaves of your indoor plants looking dull? Wipe down each leaf with a soft cloth dipped in a half-and-half mixture of warm water and milk. You'll get a nice shine, but there won't be enough residue left behind to clog the leaf pores.
Kristene Palmer, Singleton, WA.

- If your bed has wheels and moves around on the floor, place plastic coffee jar lids under the wheels – problem solved!
Miriam Hindmarsh, Mawson Lakes, SA.

- To stop drawers from sticking, rub a bar of soap across the runners to make them glide more smoothly.
Lucille Wallace, Lakes Entrance, Vic.

- Every time I opened the cupboard to get my vacuum cleaner, the hose would always fall out onto me. By screwing two tool clips to the wall, which fit the hose perfectly, the hose now stays where it's supposed to.
Glenda Mann, Mackay, Qld.

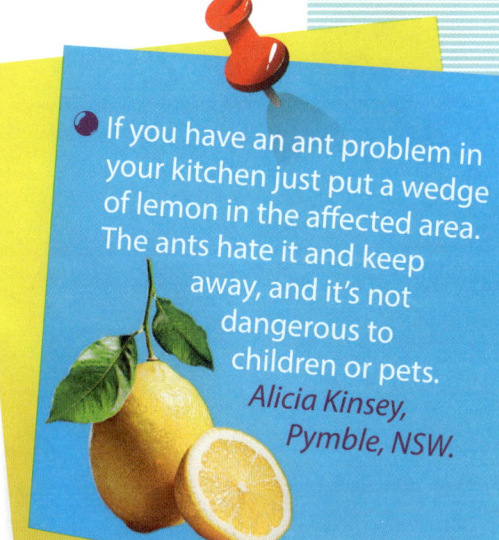

- Keep a designated drawer for odd socks. Whenever you find one, add it to the drawer and then, every few weeks, you can go through it and match everything up again.
Roy Green, Picton, NSW.

- Reduce the clutter on your bedside table by hanging a multi-pocket shoe tidy beside the bed. It's great for storing books, glasses, pens and other items, plus looks much tidier.
Sylvester Bailey, Cooma, NSW.

- If you have an ant problem in your kitchen just put a wedge of lemon in the affected area. The ants hate it and keep away, and it's not dangerous to children or pets.
Alicia Kinsey, Pymble, NSW.

Always lower the lid of your toilet seat before flushing to stop a plume of invisible bacteria from entering the air every time you flush.
Lisa Hodgetts, West Kempsey, NSW.

INDOOR LIVING

12 PAINTING TIPS

- Quickly touch-up blemishes on painted walls by dabbing on paint with an old scrunched up sock. It dries with the same dappled effect as a roller, but without the messy clean up afterwards.
Sam Nicholson, Yanchep, WA.

- It's always handy to store portions of household paint in small jars for pesky touch-up jobs. Don't forget to label the jars with the relevant paint colour.
Kris Palmer, Singleton, WA.

- Stretch a rubber band around the outside of a paint can, before you seal the can, at the level of the remaining paint. You can then see how much is left at a later date.
P. Morgan, Port Macquarie, NSW.

- Remove any lumps from a tin of paint by putting an old nylon stocking over the top and straining into another container.
C. Bebb, Kenwick, WA.

To clean paintbrushes, bring some cheap white vinegar to the boil, immerse paint brushes and let simmer for five minutes. Wash in soapy water.
Aaron Simpson, Osborne Park, WA.

- A washed out takeaway coffee cup makes a great disposable paint container.
Marjorie Smith, Bli Bli, Qld.

- To remove the smell in a freshly painted room, place half an onion cut-side up in a bowl of water. Leave it in the room overnight and the odour will disappear by morning. Throw out the onion after use.
Luke Watts, Menai, NSW.

12 PAINTING TIPS

- Painting a line at the paint level on the outside of the can will help you see the paint colour and how much is left.
Rhiannon Markson, via email.

- When you've finished washing your paintbrushes, soak them in fabric softener and then rinse – it will keep them from going hard and look as good a new.
Mavis Janetzki, Horsham, Vic.

- Use canvas drop cloths rather than plastic while painting as the thick canvas stays in place, so you don't need to tape it, and you can use it to cover any surface. Plastic drop cloths are slippery to walk on.
Brian Nielsen, Alexandria, NSW.

- A soup ladle is great for transferring paint from a large paint tin into a smaller container. This way, you won't have to lift the heavy tin and there'll be no drips.
Gwen Henderson, via email.

When painting, instead of wiping your brush against the side of the paint can and getting it all gunky, place a thick rubber band so it sits across the opening and wipe the brush on that instead.
Sharon Goodare, Waiuku, NZ.

INDOOR LIVING

105

TRAVEL

TRAVEL

TRAVEL

● Three months beforehand, airlines tend to know if their flights are going to be full, so will adjust final fares. Ask to be put on mailing lists with specific airlines or travel companies such as Flight Centre, so they can inform you when prices drop.
Janice Feeney, Bulli, NSW.

● Trawl the internet before you go and you can print out free or discount coupons for heaps of things from coffee or breakfast to entertainment and many kids' attractions.
Kay Yeung, Melbourne, Vic.

● A large food cover is a perfect way to keep any flies or creepy crawlies away from a newborn baby when you go on camping trips.
Angie Taylor, Marsden, Qld.

● Long weekends, school holidays and summertime will put room and cabin rates up. So make the most of Australia's mild winters and take a trip in the off-season.
Mary Markinson, Petersham, NSW.

● When you're travelling with kids, keep some essentials on hand at all times. Puzzle books and audio books will keep them happy, and take a well-stocked bag of fruit for healthy snacks.
Ursula Townsend, Harris Park, NSW.

- Collect shampoo product samples from magazines and take them with you when you go on holidays. It will save you both space and weight in your bag.
Edith Stanley, Gladstone, Qld.

KATHLEEN TRIES IT OUT!

WACKY BUT IT WORKS

If you love entertaining but are tight on money, reuse your teabags while making everyone a cuppa. Most people like their tea weak anyway.

- Invest in some small plastic bottles with airtight lids, available from chemists and discount stores, and decant everyday essentials like shampoo, soap, conditioner and moisturiser into them. They're much lighter and easier to pack than the full-size bottles.
Anna Holmes, East Hills, NSW.

- Eat lots of Vegemite before you go camping – mozzies won't want to go near you!
Nelson Vega, Victoria Park, WA.

- If you're travelling interstate, take the time to find out when that state's public holidays are, or you could find yourself stranded with nowhere to stay.
Marjorie Ennis, Devonport, Tas.

TRAVEL

- When travelling on overnight trains, it's a good idea to secure your backpack or suitcase to a seat or rail with a chain or bike lock. You'll sleep better knowing no-one can walk off with your bag.
Lisa Hodgetts, Kempsey, NSW.

Tie a piece of brightly coloured cloth to the handle of your suitcase and you'll be able to spot it easily on the airport carousel.
Patricia Thorn, Carlton, Vic.

- When travelling and staying in accommodation with communal clotheslines, use pegs of the same bright colour so you can easily identify your washing. You'll be less likely to get confused and take other people's washing and won't leave anything behind.
Amanda Garnet, Bowen Hills, Qld.

- When travelling, a great place to keep your small items of jewellery is in a pill container as it keeps everything together and secure.
Bernice Campbell, Lismore, NSW.

- Pin your suitcase keys inside the case when not using it. No more searching high and low for misplaced padlock keys.
Brett Bowen, Bulleen, Vic.

TRAVEL

- When packing to go overseas I wrap all my gifts in clear cellophane in case they need to be checked by customs. They can see everything and the gifts stay nicely wrapped.
Casey Copeland, Mulgrave, Vic.

- When camping, it's important you don't damage the natural area using hot, soapy water. Biodegradable soap is the answer, and dispose of greywater in areas where it won't kill the greenery. Take plenty of garbage bags and be sure to recycle whatever you can, so you can leave the bush as you found it.
Sarah Kerr, Noosaville, Qld.

- When travelling, I always pack a pillowcase to put my dirty underwear and socks in. This way, it keeps them separate from the clean clothes and makes them easier to find for washing.
Viola Hale, Ballarat, Vic.

- When camping, if you haven't got enough room in your fridge for spinach or celery, just wrap it in wet newspaper and place in a plastic bag. The greens will last for up to a week and still be fresh even without refrigeration.
Michelle Rodriquez, East Sydney, NSW.

● When packing for a holiday, I always throw a few rolls of masking tap into my bag. It's useful for securing the tops of open liquid bottles on the trip home.
Kendall Anderson, Belmont, WA.

● To make packing easy for your next trip, store all your travel items, such as adaptors, money belts, neck cushions and toiletry bags, in labelled plastic storage tubs, or in your suitcases.
Lynette Ford, Bilinga, Qld.

● Take a box of solar lights on your next camping trip to place around your campsite. It will help you avoid tripping over tent ropes and your site will be easier to spot when returning from the amenities block at night.
Jan Dimarco, Kingston, Tas.

● When driving out of town, my husband and I always tune into the local radio stations. It's amazing how much you can find out about an area.
Sandra James, Heathcote, Vic.

● Make sure you tell you bank when you're going overseas so they know that you'll be making transactions in other countries and won't report suspicious behaviour.
Pamlea Moss, Canley Heights, NSW.

TRAVEL

112

KATHLEEN TRIES IT OUT!

WACKY BUT IT WORKS

Colour co-ordinate your keys by applying different nail polish to the ends. You'll never be left wondering which key is which.

- When holidaying in our caravan, we always do our cooking outside on a barbecue, so I use the oven for extra storage space.
  Amanda Burroughs, Coonawarra, NT.

- Cook up some fried rice at home and freeze it in containers for when you're away camping. All you need to do is reheat it in a billy and you have a yummy meal.
  Jodie Fletcher, Gordon, ACT.

- When hiring a car on holidays, take a photo of the registration number using your mobile as soon as you pick it up. This helps you to easily identify the right car as most of them tend to look the same.
  S. Tanmahapran, Bentleigh, Vic.

TRAVEL

113

12 TIPS FOR PACKING THE PERFECT SUITCASE

● Make sure you know what your holiday is going to involve – formal dinners, hiking or watersports? – and pack accordingly.
Harry Jones, Peakhurst, NSW.

● Find out what the weather is like at your destination, so you're not forced to buy more suitable clothes to match the different climate.
Penny Habib, Subiaco, WA.

● Leave space in your case if you plan to shop. Overfilling cases spoils your clothes and also makes the bags too heavy.
Gwendoline Ling, Coolangatta, Qld.

● When travelling, reuse the tiny zip-lock bags that extra buttons come in to store jewellery in your suitcase.
Tara Connor, Launceston, Tas.

● Make a list to prevent doubling up on items. You don't want to end up with five white singlets and no shoes.
Frederick Parker, Drummoyne, NSW.

● Place heavy items, such as jeans and jackets at the bottom as the lining. As well as giving you an idea of how much space you have left, they'll protect your valuables.
Luella Thorn, Kellyville, NSW.

TRAVEL

- Pack shoes in plastic bags to prevent marks on clothes.
Kathleen Croft, Geelong, Vic.

- Shoes can take up a lot of space so try to minimise the number of pairs you pack. And never pack new shoes you haven't worn in yet.
June Walker, East Hills, NSW.

- Help your bras maintain their shape while also saving space by stacking bras on top of each other, folding them in half, and tucking your underwear inside.
Alex Vamos, Hobart, Tas.

Did you know? Rolling instead of folding items into a bag takes up much less space and prevents creases
Di Solomon, via email.

- To avoid spills in your bag, take lids off liquid bottles and add a layer of plastic wrap. Then when you put the lid on, use tape to seal the gap where the lid joins the container.
Virginia Gane, Casula, NSW.

- By packing a small bag of potpourri, or a scented drawer liner, you'll keep your clothes smelling sweet throughout your whole trip.
Margaret Chapman, Golden Beach, Qld.

FASHION/BEAUTY

FASHION /BEAUTY

FASHION /BEAUTY

🔴 To slash your hairdressing bill, research local beauty schools. Most will have model evenings where you can get your hair coloured or cut for a token fee. Don't be scared – most of the students doing this will be final year and there will be an eagle-eyed instructor on hand.
Ronda Day, Elizabeth, SA.

🔵 Use beeswax to waterproof canvas shoes.
Iona Little, Bowral, NSW.

🔴 To save time in the morning, choose and lay out everything you are going to wear the night before. This really helps to reduce the stress in your morning routine!
Mao Lin, South Yarra, Vic.

🔵 If the plastic handle of your blusher brush breaks, don't discard the remaining small brush. It's ideal for your make-up purse, work or travelling.
Maxine Wade, Neutral Bay, NSW.

🔴 To stop new shoes from chafing your heels, rub a plain candle against the section of shoe causing the problem. It really helps!
Rolando Sims, Perth, WA.

🔵 If your fingernails are stained after wearing dark nail polish, try scrubbing them with a little whitening toothpaste applied to a nailbrush.
Simone Faulkner, Geelong, Vic.

KATHLEEN TRIES IT OUT!

WACKY BUT IT WORKS

Don't wash your jeans, freeze them instead! Place your folded jeans into a plastic bag and pop them into the freezer. The cold temperature kills the bacteria and helps to prolong their quality. Plus, that's one less thing to wash every week.

- If you have a bracelet or watch that catches on your clothes, wrap a small piece of clear sticky tape around the catch. No-one will be able to notice and you won't risk ruining your clothes.
Esther Luna, Kensington, SA.

- Chalk is a quick-fix solution for dampness. I string a couple of pieces in my wardrobe so none of my clothes get affected by moisture.
Natasha Laurens, Bendigo, Vic.

- Attaching different colour paper clips to similar tubes of moisturiser makes it easy to pick the right one, without having to read the fine print.
Johanna Lee, Leeming, WA.

- Avoid nasty tumbles while wearing slippery shoes or slippers by sticking some small pieces of bathtub non-slip mats onto the bottom of them.
Sonja Oliver, Mandurah, WA.

FASHION/BEAUTY

● Worried about scratching your watch glass? Get a screen guard from a $2 shop – the same as you use on mobile phone screens. Cut to the shape of your watch glass and apply as you would on your phone.
Terry Kilburn, Te Hapara, NZ.

● To prolong the life of your imitation jewellery, buy a silver polishing cloth. A quick wipe over after each wear stops the tarnishing that's caused by the oil from your skin.
Jen Ferron, Shellharbour, NSW.

● I have trouble getting my feet into my shoes and find that a long ruler made of wood or plastic, placed on the heel of the shoe helps to ease my foot in.
Lucinda Parker, Faulconbridge, NSW.

● To cleanse my skin, I use two teaspoons of powdered milk, mixed with a little water to form a paste. I apply it to my face and leave it for about 10 minutes before rinsing with water. It leaves my skin feeling smooth and nourished.
Deborah Baker, Dandenong, Vic.

● When a pillowcase gets too old, I cut a small hole in the end of it and slip it over a clothes hanger to protect my clothes from dust.
Denise Scarborough, Perth, WA.

- To combat silverfish in your clothes drawers, pop a handful of cloves in a little fabric pouch together with some Epsom salts, then place the bag among your clothes.
Rachel White, Coolangatta, Qld.

- The next time you're buying make-up, ask the salesperson about end-of-line products on sale. Often companies will slash the prices to make room for newer stock that's practically identical, apart from the packaging. It's also worth asking if they have samples available.
Naomi King, Sutherland, NSW.

- If you want to avoid back and neck problems, steer clear of cheap shoes. If you've got your eye on a new pair, compare prices in small specialty shops with those of department stores, which can often sell for less.
Ashleigh Price, Broome, WA.

- If your eyes are red and puffy and you need to go out, wrap an icepack in a towel and rest it across your eyes for a few minutes. Then, using your ring finger, gently dab under your eyes to reduce the build-up of fluid and reduce puffiness.
Kara Field, Mt Annan, NSW.

- If you've found a grey hair and don't have time to go to the hairdressers, use mascara to cover it.
Lurline White, Ipswich, Qld.

FASHION/BEAUTY

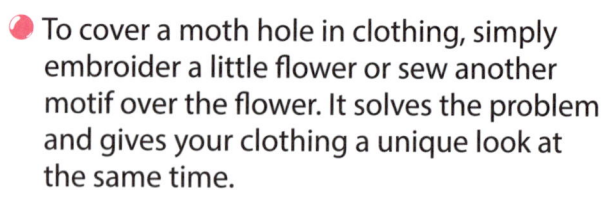

- To cover a moth hole in clothing, simply embroider a little flower or sew another motif over the flower. It solves the problem and gives your clothing a unique look at the same time.
Jean Gutierrez, via email.

- If you've got hair dye on your skin, as disgusting as it sounds, you might have to resort to an old trick used by hairdressers. Dab some damp cotton wool in cigarette ash and gently rub over the stain.
Mary Koutsis, Shoalhaven, NSW.

- If your favourite nail varnish has dried up, add a little nail polish remover to the bottle. Replace the lid, shake well and you'll get a few more coats.
Doti Hallowell, Auckland, NZ.

- If you don't have time to shampoo your hair, dry shampoo is great for these emergencies but it can be expensive. For a cheaper quick-fix, sprinkle some talcum powder on the roots of your hair, leave for a minute and then brush out. But don't be too generous unless you want to turn yourself grey!
Kathleen Norris, Bundeena, NSW.

- To remove lint from clothes and linen, run a disposable razor over the item.
Gabriela Coustas, Mawson Lakes, SA.

- When you're wearing any of the beautiful glitter tops available, spray with hairspray and you won't end up covered in glitter.
Anne-marie Ayling, Katherine, NT.

KATHLEEN TRIES IT OUT!

WACKY BUT IT WORKS

When bras get grey and boring, give them a tie-dye makeover. Just twist the bra into a sausage shape, tie on a few elastic bands and let it sit in a bowl of cold water with food colouring. Once it's dried, you have a new funky, tie-dyed bra to wear.

- Dry wet shoes quicker by stuffing them with crumpled balls of newspaper. Leave overnight for the paper to soak up the water. By morning your shoes should be dry and ready for you to wear again.
Ora Walton, South Grafton, NSW.

- Put a piece of chalk in your jewellery box. It absorbs the moisture that makes the metal tarnish.
Sofie Mavidis, Patterson Lakes, Vic.

- To keep necklaces untangled, run each of them through a straw, cut the straw to the appropiate length and close the chain clasp before storing away. The chains will always be ready to wear with no knots.
Leticia Krichmar, Carlton, Vic.

- Empty chocolate boxes are great for keeping your earrings in, as the empty compartments keep them separated and easy to find.
Penny Ngyuen, Canberra, ACT.

FASHION/BEAUTY

123

● To waterproof leather boots or shoes, rub with Vaseline or chest rub, then use a dry cloth to remove.
Dolores Maalouf, North Sydney, NSW.

● To clean dust off suede shoes, use some sticky tape or masking tape. Just place the tape over the shoes, then remove. The dust will stick to the tape and leave your shoes clean.
Alli Moore, Launceston, Tas.

● To soften dry, hard heels, rub petroleum jelly over them, then put on thick cotton socks and leave overnight.
Analiese Fidler, Port Adelaide, SA.

● To stop your razor blades from going rusty, soak in baby oil – this not only stops rusting, but the blades will last longer and be smoother on the skin.
Kania Connor, Ottoway, SA.

● If you need to dry nail polish in a hurry, spray with olive oil spray, leave for 30 seconds then rinse.
Julietta Leduc, Perth, WA.

● When you have washed your hair, rinse with lemon juice and water. It gives a real shine and smells great, too.
Laina Ortega, Golden Beach, Qld.

- Wrap a banana skin over warts using a bandage and leave in place overnight. Within two to three days the warts should disappear.
Pat Bishop, Chatswood, NSW.

- Make your own facial scrub by adding a teaspoon of sugar to your normal cleanser and massage into your face as usual. For a coarser texture, add raw sugar.
Ashly Bailey, Cartwright, NSW.

- If your eyeliner and lipliner pencils break when being sharpened, try freezing them first. The crayon in the pencils will remain firm, so you get a nice sharp point.
Annemarie Pellegrini, Mascot, NSW.

- Make-up remover wipes can cost a fortune, so a quick and cheaper option is to use baby wipes. They work just as well for half the price.
Alex Rielly, Campbelltown, NSW.

If you have sensitive skin, don't waste money on expensive products, use baby shampoo, soap and oil. These products are especially made for babies who have very sensitive skin.
Laurene Coover, Parafield Gardens, SA.

- Go through your clothes every six months and donate to charity anything you haven't worn in a year. This means your clothes have more room to hang properly – air needs to circulate around them to prevent that musty smell.
Lee Wesson, Wagga Wagga, NSW.

- To make nail polish stay on nails longer, first coat fingernails with white vinegar using a cotton ball. Let dry then apply nail polish.
Mellisa Ostrowski, Mt Hotham, Vic.

- Don't put dirty clothes back in your wardrobe – moths are attracted to sweat and food on clothes, not the fabric itself.
Marget Osborne, Albury, NSW.

- Pour some bicarbonate of soda into smelly shoes and leave for two to three days to absorb the odour, then vacuum up.
Emma Farrow, Buderim, Qld.

- If you don't want to throw away your old woolly beanies, cut holes for a spout and handle to turn them into tea-cosies.
Kerry Astill, Jindabyne, NSW.

KATHLEEN TRIES IT OUT!

WACKY BUT IT WORKS

- To prevent buttons from becoming loose or undone, dab a little clear nail varnish on the top thread or onto the stem of the thread and leave to dry.

- If your new shoes are too tight, put the nozzle of your hairdryer into the shoe and turn on low. When the shoe gets warm, stuff with newspaper or socks to stretch it.
Marleen Bashir, Bairnsdale, Vic.

- Underpants with the leg holes sewn up make great hats.
Myrtle Cooper, Bathurst, NSW.

- To remove a bandaid painlessly, rub it with baby oil and allow the oil to soak in for a couple of minutes before removing.
Jackie Sutherland, Randwick, NSW.

- To help restore puffy eyes to normal, pour a little milk onto cotton wool and dab over the eye.
Aurelia James, Newcastle, NSW.

FASHION/BEAUTY

- I'm a hairdresser and have a good tip for women going to get their hair done – always wear a button-down top, so you don't mess up your style if you're changing and going out for the evening.
Debbie Bowden, Katoomba, NSW.

If your skin is looking dry and flaky, toss a handful of orange peel into your bath. The peel infuses the water with natural oils that help moisturise the skin, and the scent of citrus will leave you feeling refreshed.
Nicole Prince, Scarborough, Qld.

- To prolong the life of your silver-plated jewellery, buy a silver polishing cloth from the supermarket. A quick wipe over after each wear stops the tarnishing that is caused by the oil on your skin.
Eileen Clarke, Adelaide, SA.

- Store your fashion hats by putting scrunched-up cellophane in the crown, with enough coming out the bottom so it doesn't rest on the brim. This helps keep them in perfect shape until you wear them next.
Sandy Williamson, Deakin, ACT.

- Turn unwanted dangling hook earrings into beautiful key chains. Simply thread through the hole in a key, bend into a circle with pliers and twist to secure.
*Fiona Olson,
Tin Can Bay, Qld.*

- If you often lose the buttons on your clothes, use colourless fishing line to sew them on – the buttons never come off.
Jecinta Day, Marrickville, NSW.

- Pour a cup of powdered milk under the running tap while filling your bath. Powdered milk is inexpensive compared to luxury bath products, and will leave you with silk soft skin.
Christina Hatzis, Yokine, WA.

- To store hairclips, attach a long piece of ribbon to a small piece of wood or cardboard and decorate it, as desired. Clip the hairclips onto the ribbon and hang it up.
Sarah Tanmahapran, Bentleigh, Vic.

- Mix a cupful of oatmeal with a little water and rub through oily or grimy hands to instantly clean.
Diana Horsefield, Gosford, NSW.

- If an item of your clothing has shoulder pads that you've removed, don't throw them away. Stitch or safety pin the pads to the ends of your clothes hangers to help keep your jackets and shirts in good shape.
Margaret Ainslie, Sunshine, Vic.

- To make your finger nails stronger, put a slice of garlic into your nail polish bottle.
Rachel Jaynoy, Tumut, NSW.

- To stop your garments from fading, always turn your clothes inside out when hanging on the line.
M. Glass, Engadine, NSW.

- Before dying your hair, apply Vaseline near and around your hairline, behind your ears and the nape of your neck. This will prevent the dye staining skin and will wash off in the shower.
Paige Rogers, Mount Gambier, SA.

- To make your perfume last all night, rub a little Vaseline on your wrists and neck before applying it.
Anne Bianco, Castle Hill, NSW.

- During summer, keep your eyeliner pencils in the fridge to stop them from going soft.
Audrey Peter, Carrolup, WA.

WACKY BUT IT WORKS

- Use excess eye cream on cuticles. The more you hydrate your cuticles, the stronger your nails will be.
Dolores Curry, Acton, WA.

- Apply tea tree oil to a pimple or break out as soon as you spot it. It will help clear skin up in no time.
Velma Fowler, Wollongong, NSW.

- My husband bought me a set of Russian dolls. They sat on my coffee table for weeks, until I realised I could use them as individual jewellery boxes. Now all my rings, necklaces and bracelets are kept in different dolls!
Liz Jennings, Kensington Park, SA.

- A stylish way to keep your hats organised and on display, is to attach them to a corkboard and hang it in your office or even in the bedroom. It's easy to do and looks like a contemporary artwork.
Eva Neal, Moree, NSW.

- Clean your make-up brushes by soaking them in a tablespoon of white vinegar in a cup of hot water for about 20 minutes. Follow this with a hot, then cold rinse and pat dry. This will disinfect and dissolve any grease or make-up on the brushes.
Nettie Carr, Rockhampton, Qld.

To make sure you drink enough water every day, label your bottle with different hours and make sure you reach the mark by the hour.

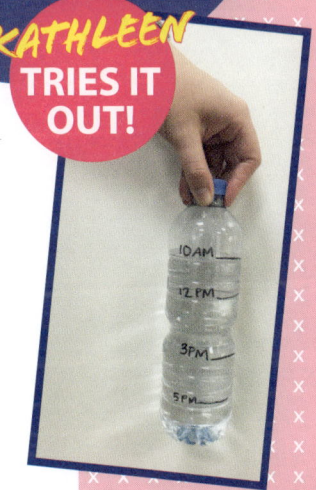

KATHLEEN TRIES IT OUT!

FASHION/BEAUTY

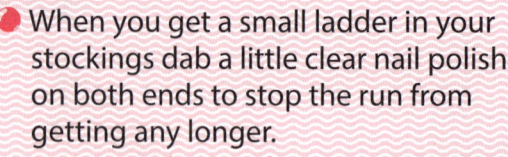

- When you get a small ladder in your stockings dab a little clear nail polish on both ends to stop the run from getting any longer.
Leticia Drake, Strathmore, Vic.

- Use your leftover bits of wool to make colourful bed socks. Patterns are easily found online and in many knitting books – they look great and keep your nice and warm!
Mary Carter, Nairne, SA.

- A great colourant for slightly greying hair is natural henna conditioner. It gives your hair a lovely natural shine and you can buy it at a reasonable price from most health food shops.
Charlotte Beck, Innaloo, WA.

- When putting on a light-coloured top, I put it on over my head back-to-front and then turn it around the right way – no more make-up marks ruining the front of my clothes.
Kerry Collins, Moss Vale, NSW.

By mixing a little Vaseline with your favourite blush and a few drops of vanilla essential oil, this makes a fabulous, yet much cheaper lip gloss that smells delicious!
Nicole Benson, Rokeby, Tas.

- Stop your scarf from slipping off your neck by overlapping the ends and securing with your favourite brooch.
Danielle Harmer, Highgate Hill, Qld.

- To make pantihose last longer, soak them for 30 minutes in a solution of ½ cup of salt water to 8 cups of water. Then rinse with cool water before drying and wearing. This makes them more resistant to snagging and laddering.
Denise Reese, Bulli, NSW.

- To help your handbag retain its shape when it's not in use, pack it with plastic bags or newspaper.
Gemma Beverly, Woodvale, WA.

- Instead of buying shoe containers to store your shoes, take a photo of the shoes and glue it onto the box that the shoes came in. Then you can see at a glance what's in the shoe box.
Delese Bonser, Greenwood, WA.

- Instead of going and buying the waterproof spray for your leather shoes, spray WD40 on a cloth and wipe over the shoe, then buff with a soft clean cloth to shine. A cheap and easy way to make your new shoes waterproof!
Katrina Oliver, Fyshwick, ACT.

- If you don't have nail polish remover, apply clear nail polish over your nail, and then wipe off. It will remove old polish.
Myrtle Meyer, Wallal, WA.

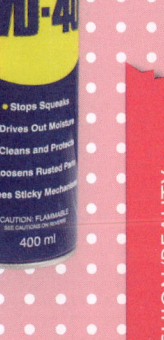

FASHION/BEAUTY

133

Use cardboard shoeboxes as dividers to keep your underwear drawers neat and tidy. Saves time when you need to get dressed by making everything accessible and easy to find.
Karen Palmer, Ipswich, Qld.

● Plastic shower rings hooked through a crocheted coat hanger is a great invention for hanging your scarves on.
Rosie Smith, Goulburn, NSW.

● I always wear a pair of disposable dishwashing gloves when putting on stockings, to prevent making holes in them.
Natalie Elliot, Barton, ACT.

● Freeze your eyeliner 15 minutes prior to applying make-up. It glides along the lash line much more easily and seamlessly without crumbling.
Natalie Moore, Helensburgh, NSW.

● A smile is an inexpensive way to immediately improve your looks!
Lisa Farrington, Canberra, ACT.

KATHLEEN TRIES IT OUT!

WACKY BUT IT WORKS

Need to iron your collar? Just use a hair straightener.

- For a natural, inexpensive and effective facial cleanser, simply mix bran with a little warm milk to form a creamy mixture. Apply to the face and gently massage in, then rinse off with lukewarm water. It works a charm!
Doris Connor, Launceston, Tas.

- When shopping for new glasses, take along a friend and a digital camera or phone. Get your friend to snap you wearing a few favourite frames, then look at the photos when you get home. This way you'll select frames that you suit you with no pressure from sales staff.
Maureen Knowles, Canberra, ACT.

- If you're undecided about a purchase, attach the receipt to the tag with a paperclip. If you decide to return it, everything you need is in one spot.
Rachael Witt, Fremantle, WA.

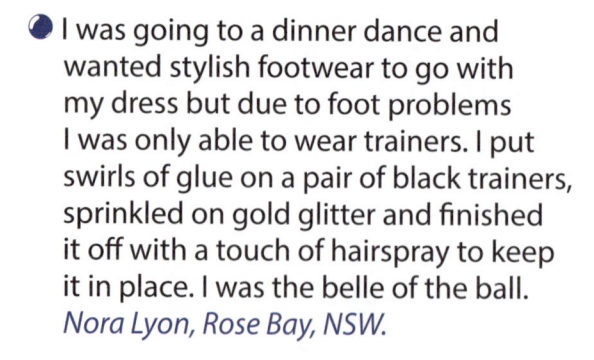

● I was going to a dinner dance and wanted stylish footwear to go with my dress but due to foot problems I was only able to wear trainers. I put swirls of glue on a pair of black trainers, sprinkled on gold glitter and finished it off with a touch of hairspray to keep it in place. I was the belle of the ball.
Nora Lyon, Rose Bay, NSW.

● When pressing a pleated skirt, I slide bobby pins onto the folds at the hem to keep the pleats in place as I iron.
Tralisa Jarvis, Hermit Park, Qld.

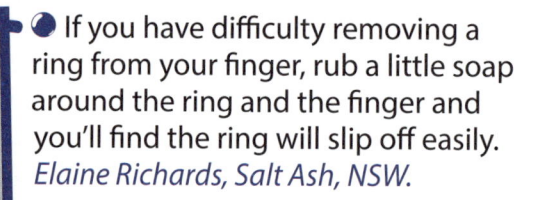

● If you have difficulty removing a ring from your finger, rub a little soap around the ring and the finger and you'll find the ring will slip off easily.
Elaine Richards, Salt Ash, NSW.

● Spray leave-in conditioner onto a hairbrush before styling hair to prevent flyaways.
Elaine Turner, South West Rocks, NSW.

● If you have pieces of gold jewellery that are broken or never worn, ask a jeweller to melt them down and create something you'll want to wear and cherish.
Yvette Rydman, Higgins, ACT.

● When I can no longer get any product out of my cosmetics, I cut the packaging open and transfer any remaining product into small airtight containers. This way I get heaps more life out of them.
Karlee Jones, Rockingham, WA.

Keep boots upright by cutting a pool noodle to length and placing inside each boot – cardboard cylinders from cling wrap would also work.
Margaret Potts, Rivett, ACT.

- To cover up roots in a hurry, use a dry shampoo spray that matches your hair colour.
  Carol Tomlinson, Labrador, Qld.

- Use a thin lip brush to retrieve the last bits of lipstick from an old stick of lipstick – you'll be surprised how much is left.
  Wilma Winter, Kedron, Qld.

- To clean combs and hairbrushes, simply soak for several minutes in ¼ cup hot water and two tablespoons baking soda. Rinse and pat dry.
  Chris Walton, Ferny Hills, Qld.

- Make diamonds and other precious jewels sparkle by brushing with toothpaste and rinsing in clean cold water.
  Marie T. Matheson, Emu Plains, NSW.

FASHION/BEAUTY

THE GREAT OUTDOORS

THE GREAT OUTDOORS

THE GREAT OUTDOORS

139

THE GREAT OUTDOORS

🍊 We get lots of leaves on our front doorstep around autumn so I plug in an extension cord and use my vacuum to suck them all up. Then I dump them in the compost bin.
Tahlia Bourke, Toowoomba, Qld.

🟢 Don't overfill a space with furniture. There's nothing more claustrophobic than a cluttered garden. You can always keep spare folding chairs packed away for extra guests – and keep overhanging or high trees and bushes trimmed back.
Harriet Jackson, Wodonga, NSW.

🍊 Each time you crack an egg open, put the shell in a container in the fridge. When the container is full, crush the shells into small bits and sprinkle them around the base of your plants. The sharp shells help keep the slugs, snails and other bugs away and add a touch of calcium to the soil.
Velma Gonzales, Northampton, WA.

KATHLEEN TRIES IT OUT!

WACKY BUT IT WORKS

When you're given flowers and can't find a vase to fit them, use an old tennis ball canister. It works perfectly. Add some decorations for a personal touch if you like. No need to splash out on a vase ever again.

🍊 No patio? No problem! Invest in a few rubber or plastic-backed outdoor rugs. They're inexpensive and make for perfect picnic-style evenings with friends.
Holli Vautin, Swan Hill, NSW.

🍏 Plan ahead and buy garden furniture in winter sales. You'll get some great deals and could save hundreds of dollars.
Charline An, Maryborough, Qld.

🍊 If your old wheelbarrow has holes in it, line it with wire mesh, then shade cloth. Fill with potting mix and plants for a lovely portable garden bed.
Harvey Ortega, Dee Why, NSW.

THE GREAT OUTDOORS

● When planting tomato plants in tubs, also include a basil plant because this helps to keep green and black flies away.
Tamara Mills, Healesville, Vic.

● Instead of throwing out old wine glasses with broken bases, stick them around the garden and use them as candle holders.
Gail Perkins, via email.

● Help prevent your gutters from blocking up with leaves by covering them with chicken wire.
Sandy Mcdonald, Collinsville, Qld.

● When you're going fishing, take an ironing board with you to scale and fillet the fish on. It makes things much easier, it's portable and you can simply wash the whole thing down when you're finished.
Jennifer Schneider, Pemberton, WA.

● To keep your picnic tablecloth from blowing away on a windy day, sew pockets at the corners and add small weights, such as stones or pebbles.
Kendall Mack, Adelaide, SA.

- To make a garlic or chilli spray that stops possums eating your plants, place two tablespoons of freshly crushed garlic or finely chopped hot chilli into one litre of hot water. Allow to stand overnight.
Marguerite Campbell, Fosterton, NSW.

- If you have problems with flies while eating outside, buy a pack of fly swats and hang them on hooks attached to a fishing line over your table. If you get a slight breeze they'll move and the flies won't land on the plates or your guests.
Gail Greener, Anna Bay, NSW.

- Instead of throwing out old newspapers, roll them up tightly and secure with twine. Store them somewhere dry and when winter rolls around they will make great firelighters if you're out of kindling.
Joyce Reeves, Canning Vale, WA.

- To help you carry drinks through a crowd or to a picnic, put your cups in deep muffin trays. The muffin holes will keep the cup steady, and if they spill, the muffin tray will catch all the drips.
Tamara Suthington, Wamberal, NSW.

- If your hanging baskets don't have flat bottoms, sit them in a bucket when filling with plants – this makes them steady and easier to fill.
Pat Baker, Fingal Bay, NSW.

THE GREAT OUTDOORS

- It's important to keep your patio tiles clean and free of moss. As well as being unsightly, stained tiles get harder to clean the longer they're left, plus they're expensive and difficult to replace. Invest in a hard bristle garden brush – you can pick them up cheaply at hardware stores or garden centres.
Keith Harold, Newport, NSW.

- When planting up tubs, instead of putting stones into the bottom, put a square of absorbent material, such as Chux cloth. This cloth will still provide drainage, but will also stop small slugs getting in and eating the new plants.
Raelene Foster, Darwin, NT.

- If your roses are being attacked by black flies, place two or three squirts of soap in a spray bottle with a litre of water. Spray plants liberally with this mixture. It's environmentally friendly and not harmful to pets, children or 'good' insects, such as ladybirds.
Marion Little, Kilmore, Vic.

- Salt, boiling water and vinegar are all natural, inexpensive weed killers.
Monty Richardson, Torquay, Vic.

KATHLEEN TRIES IT OUT!

WACKY BUT IT WORKS

If you spend hours on your knees planting and gardening and notice your knees are becoming increasingly uncomfortable, grab an old padded bra, cut it in half and use the cups as cushioned kneepads.

- Lightly spray mineral turps on any unwanted green shoots in the garden and you'll see results within 24 hours.
Ron Rose, St. Clair, NSW.

- Instead of rocks, use leftover styrofoam packing as drainage in the bottom of plant pots.
Deborah Bowden, Rosebud, Vic.

- Place a thermometer inside your esky to ensure you keep food at the right temperature if you're heading out for a picnic.
Lisa Hodgetts, West Kempsey, NSW.

- Dig banana skins into the soil around flowers to fertilise them with sulphur, sodium, calcium, magnesium, phosphorous and silica.
Marilyn Parks, Forbes, NSW.

- Always keep a can of WD-40 handy to clean your garden tools after every use.
Peter Hilliard, Ballina, NSW.

THE GREAT OUTDOORS

- When looking after seedling trays and small pot plants, use a recycled pop-top drink bottle. The small spout is ideal as it doesn't spill or waste any water.
Samantha Wilson, Wagga Wagga, NSW.

- If you wear reading glasses, keep a spare pair in the shed/garage so you can read the instructions on your seed packs and new plants.
Lucas Johnson, Castlemaine, Vic.

- Consider greywater recycling. Divert water from your washing machine, shower, laundry tub, etc., onto your garden and you could save up to 400L of fresh water a day.
Lillian Savidis, Burleigh Heads, Qld.

- Cover your pool when not in use and this will reduce water evaporation by up to 90 per cent.
Grant Townsend, Willowbank, Qld.

- Glass coffee lids make super-handy containers for sauces if you're having a barbecue.
Beryl Thomas, St Kilda, Vic

- Keep used tea bags to put around indoor plants if you're going to be away. Place in the pot away from the plant stem and water well. The more tea bags you put around, the longer the pot stays moist.
Jan Herman, Broadford, Vic.

- Don't cut your grass too short. Longer lawns survive better and recover faster from periods of very dry weather.
Freddy Stamos, Woodend, Vic.

- During our trips to caravan parks we often find the barbecues aren't very clean. Our solution is to place a sheet of non-stick baking paper on the hotplate. Meat and chicken cook perfectly this way and we can just throw the paper away afterwards. No more cleaning up!
Vicki Druin, Tewantin, Qld.

- Attach a strip of luminous tape to your torch. This will make it easier to find in the event of a blackout.
Trish Wallace, Adelaide North, SA.

- To help create the perfect picnic setting, sew curtain rings to the corner of a picnic rug and peg it to the ground using tent pegs. This stops it from blowing away.
Nerida Bakker, Cairns, Qld.

- If your garlic starts to sprout, put the sprouting cloves in a pot and let them grow. The green shoots taste a lot stronger than the cloves – chop them up and add to salads.
Christine Manning, Salamander Bay, NSW.

THE GREAT OUTDOORS

● Dip plant cuttings in honey before planting to ensure good growth.
Lois Kearns, Medowie, NSW.

● Before using the barbecue, wipe down the grill with cooking oil to prevent food from sticking.
Maureen Buckley, Noble Park, Vic.

● If your stubby holders are always going astray, why not make a 'holder' for them. A few planks of wood with Velcro attached make a great storage spot for stubby holders.
Annie Brandes, Marcoola, Qld.

● To keep slugs and snails out of your potted plants, smear some petroleum jelly on the outside of the pots.
Diane Harwood, Brunswick, Vic.

● Planting garlic in between your roses is an eco-friendly way of keeping the dreaded green fly at bay.
Steven Taunton, Killara, NSW.

● Make your own slow-release fertiliser. Mix coffee grounds with tea bags and a little soil. This makes great compost and is a wonderful fertiliser you can put around your prize plants.
Angela Babic, Perth, WA.

WACKY BUT IT WORKS

When travelling, even if it's just an overnight trip, keep your jewellery in an old glasses case. It snaps shut, won't open and holds all tiny jewels tight and safe.

- To keep spiders and other insects out of your gardening gloves, secure the tops with a rubber band when they're not in use.
Annie Brandes, Marcoola, Qld.

- Onions stunt the growth of beans and wood ash is a great repellent for keeping bugs and white butterflies away from cabbage, broccoli and cauliflower plants. Soapy water usually cures sooty mould in the early stages and planting nasturtiums in or near your vegetable garden will deter many pests.
Gwen Deem, Cougal, NSW.

- Soak seeds, especially vegetable seeds, before planting in a weak solution of liquid fertiliser. It aids germination.
Cath Burges, Bunbury, WA.

THE GREAT OUTDOORS

🟠 Sprinkle sawdust around your plants to keep snails at bay.
Penny Dominelli, Blakehurst, NSW.

🟢 If entertaining outside, protect your food from bugs by cutting a lime in half and covering it in cloves. Bugs hate it.
S. Smith, Mt Gambier, SA.

🟠 Ground cinnamon spread on doorways will stop ants from coming into your home.
Christina Hatzis, Yokine, WA.

🟢 To avoid heat stress damaging your plants during the summer months, re-pot plants into bigger pots. This will increase the water-holding capacity around their roots.
D. Cardell, Merimbula, NSW.

🟠 If you have an outside gas heater, place your pots of plant clippings on top. The warmth of the heater helps the roots grow faster.
Brenda Janson, Buderim, Qld.

🟢 If you have an area in your garden that just won't grow any plants, build a bench seat instead. It looks great!
Suzanne Warmington, Lyons, ACT.

🟠 Each time you change the water of your fish tank, save the water and use it to water your house plants. It's full of nutrients and makes a great fertiliser.
Ada Ramirez, Nunyle Hall, WA.

🟢 Mint is the easiest herb to grow, as it loves water and isn't dependent on sunlight.
Eliza Wetherspoon, Werona, Vic.

Keep your car windows ice and frost-free this winter by mixing three parts vinegar to one part water and putting it in a spray bottle. Spray onto the windows as needed.
Sophie Ballard, Shailer Park, Qld.

- When mowing you're lawn, don't look down – you'll mow much straighter if you focus about three metres ahead of the mower rather than directly at the wheels.
Charles Floyd, Avalon, NSW.

- If you have black tyre marks on your driveway, they will lift right off if you spray mozzie repellent on them – amazing but true!
Virgil Spencer, Broome, WA.

- Around two litres of cold water comes through my kitchen tap while I'm waiting for it to become hot. I collect this in empty milk containers and use it to water my plants around the house. It's a great way to save water and all you need is a milk container.
Debra Seegers, Stanwell, Vic.

- If you're allowed to burn off to clear your yard, use a cylinder drum from an old washing machine. It's much more effective and safer than burning leaves on the ground.
Nicola Francis, Ravenswood, Tas.

- Turn punctured unfixable balls into hanging plant basket liners. Simply cut the ball in half, line an empty basket with the balls and fill with soil and the plant.
Tracy Vega, Ilarwill, NSW.

THE GREAT OUTDOORS

🟠 A cheap way of getting rid of ants that doesn't involve spaying your home with harsh chemicals is to chop a handful of fresh red chillies and grate half a bar of pure soap. Put both in a spray bottle with water and shake before use. The ants hate it!
Salvador Terry, Campbelltown, NSW.

🟢 If you have a smelly wheelie bin, sprinkle some fresh kitty litter in the bottom of it. This keeps the bin odour-free and it'll be tipped out when collected by the garbage truck.
Juanita Baker, Belmont, WA.

🟠 If you forgot to chill party drinks before your guests arrived, place the bottles in a large pot and cover with as much ice as possible. Fill with water and mix in two cups of salt. The drinks will be ice cold within two minutes.
Rosie Beaton, Augustine Heights, Qld.

When potting plants, place a coffee filter in the bottom of the pot over the drainage holes. This will help to prevent the soil draining out.
Toni Gross, Smoky Bay, SA.

🟢 Save the salty water from boiled potatoes and pour it over the stubborn weeds in your outdoor pavers. The combination of starch and salt water makes an excellent organic weed killer.
Sergio Sheffler, Mapleton, Qld.

🟠 Pour cooking oil into recycled plastic sauce bottles, for easy mess-free use at your barbecue.
Henrietta Kleim, Wavell Heights, Qld.

THE GREAT OUTDOORS

- During the colder weather protect your more delicate plants from frost by placing cardboard boxes over them. It works perfectly and is a simple and inexpensive solution.
Marion Guerrero, Somerville, Vic.

- If you have a Colorbond fence that looks faded, rubbing it over with a rag with a bit of diesel on it once a year makes it look like new.
Julie Campbell, Hazelbrook, NSW.

- Avoid the dirty task of cleaning your wheelie bin by turning it upside down and placing over the top of a sprinkler.
Hattie Jacobson, Dunlop, ACT.

- If you have a pool, check and clean the skimmer basket and hair and lint pot basket weekly to ensure it stays clean.
Bob Frances, Rapid Creek, NT.

- An old umbrella stand makes a perfect place to hold your garden rake.
Russell Haines, Herveys Range, Qld.

- Turn your empty tins into a herb garden, by simply filling with soil and planting herbs of choice.
Madison Green, Charles Stuart, SA.

WACKY BUT IT WORKS

Keep wet face washers in the fridge during the warmer months. That way, if you've been out in the garden and are overheating, you can cool down easily.

THE GREAT OUTDOORS

I made a palette planter from an old palette I had laying around. I used some leftover paint and a scrap piece of wood to make a sign, then added some plants I had in pots. It only cost me $10 to make, looks fantastic in my garden and it's a great way to use up materials that would otherwise have ended up at the tip.
Mia Chamberlain, via email.

- Free blocked drains by pouring one jug of boiling water down it, followed by half a cup of baking soda and half a cup of white vinegar. When it stops bubbling, pour one more jug of boiling water down.
Sheryl Whittington, Kensington Park, SA.

- I place a recycling plastic bag in my laundry trolley when I am tidying up any pot plants or shrubs that are at waist height to put all the weeds and dead leaves in. That way I don't have to keep bending down to the ground to pick up any bits and pieces I have trimmed or weeded, and I can also push my laundry trolley around while doing my trimming from plant to plant.
Daphne Harrison, Townsville, Qld.

- To prevent caterpillars from eating your plants, spray them with a mixture of one part vinegar, three parts water, a dash of dishwashing liquid and a pinch of chilli!
Amy Jerkins, Bowen Hills, Qld.

- Make your neighbours think you have a fancy fireplace by keeping a soot shovel outside your front door.
L. Graham, Alfredton, Vic.

- Paint the handles of your gardens tools a bright, colour other than green to help you find them among your plants.
Teresa Grice, Brisbane, Qld.

- Over-watering plants is worse than under watering. It is easier to revive a dry plant than try to dry out drowned roots.
Diane Strong, Tuross Head, NSW.

- If you are feeling depressed, plant a pot. Put it where you will see it lots, like on your front doorstep or outside your kitchen window. You will not believe how a mini garden will lift your spirits when you are feeling down.
K. Simpson, Carlton, Vic.

MONEY SAVING

MONEY SAVING

MONEY SAVING

- Take advantage of two-for-one promotions on items that don't go out of date, products such as toothpaste and shampoo.
Nora Killcare, Lindfield, NSW.

- I save water while in the shower by singing along to my favourite song and once the tune is finished, I turn the taps off.
Suellen Sockwell, Carramar, NSW.

- Local papers and phone directories are a great source for wholesaler butchers, clothing and health products. There are also lots of coupons for eating out cheaply.
Beverly Hudson, Lower Cudgera, NSW.

- Keep a picture of something that you are saving for in your wallet or purse. This will serve as reminder to not make unnecessary purchases to help get what you are saving for sooner.
M. Taylor, Bossley Park, NSW.

Cut your dishwasher tablets in half – your dishes will be just as clean, and shining as if you'd used a whole tablet.
Paul Chan, Fremantle, WA.

- At specialist stores that you use regularly, such as drycleaners and shoe repairers, ask for a discount even when they're not advertised. Customer loyalty is often rewarded.
Rachel Leverton, Redcliffe, Qld.

KATHLEEN TRIES IT OUT!

WACKY BUT IT WORKS

- If you love playing cards, use an upside down egg carton as a card holder. It's cheap and works just as the well as the real, more expensive ones.

- Refill your hand-washing soap pumps with children's bubble bath. It's gentle on your skin and you can buy a large bottle for a lot cheaper than normal hand wash.
Craig Adkins, Epping, Vic.

- If you want to keep some cash at home, here's a great way to hide it. Wash out an empty Vegemite jar, paint the inside black, then use it store the cash on your pantry shelves. It can't be picked from the real thing.
Myron Howell, East Perth, WA.

- Use a foam sponge when posting small fragile items. Just make a slit in one end and tuck the gift safely inside. It keeps the item safe and costs less on postage than heavier packaging.
Kristen Rodgers, Robertson, NSW.

MONEY SAVING

- Consider taking advantage of online shopping and delivery services. Although there is usually a small charge, taking away the hassle of getting to a supermarket, paying for transport and possibly parking, and the packing of goods, could mean you can make better use of your time and save cash. Some stores also include surprise free gifts!
Sherri Vickers, Oatley, NSW.

- Check your vehicle regularly. Low tyre pressure can increase your car's fuel consumption by as much as three per cent, so it pays to keep your car shipshape.
Adrienne Parker, Daylesford, Vic.

- Car air-conditioning might feel like a necessity in summer but it can increase petrol consumption. Instead, park in shaded areas and roll those windows down when driving and enjoy the cool breeze for free.
Orla Faye, Kincumber, NSW.

- Fill up your petrol on a Monday or Tuesday to save up to 10 cents a litre. Oil companies tend to raise prices towards the end of the week.
Katrina Kevic, Tamborine, Qld.

- Ask your favourite places to eat about loyalty cards, points or weekly specials. Sometimes they're not advertised, but this could cut your dining bill in half.
Ingrid Northcote, Miller, NSW.

- Spending $2.50 a day on coffee from the cafe near work? Make a plunger of coffee at work and save $50 a month. Buy yourself a cute new bag or a birthday gift for a friend instead.
Wilma Van Helsen, Gosford, NSW.

- If you can't afford curtains but need some privacy, then simply use clean shower curtains. They're much cheaper but still do the job.
Lillian Leak, Mooloolaba, Qld.

- Instead of throwing out old ceramic containers (like the one my toilet brush came in), I clean them out and put plants in them. It's cheaper than buying a potted plan.
Holly Brose, Ballarat, Vic.

- Don't throw away plastic bread clips, recycle them. They make excellent clothes pegs.
Freida Wiegold, Perth, WA.

- Spending $6 a day on a sandwich? Bring in your lunch and save $120 a month. If you make your own coffee too, you've now got $170 for some new clothes, or perhaps a meal in a swanky restaurant.
Paula Yates, Noosaville, Qld.

MONEY SAVING

- Use the microwave as often as you can as an alternative to the oven. It uses a fraction of the energy.
Molly Hilton, Petersham, NSW.

- When the batteries in your TV run remote run out, try replacing only one battery. There's often enough charge to keep the other battery going for a while and it saves you money.
Harriet Stone, Glenelg, SA.

- Here's an inexpensive present for anyone with a sweet tooth. Put some florists' foam in a nice box. Sticky tape various chocolate bars onto skewers and poke them into the box to resemble a bouquet of flowers. Add a ribbon or any other decorations you wish for a sweet gift.
Lorelei Boswell, Maroochydore, Qld.

- Keep the lids from all your hairspray and deodorant bottles, wash well and use them for kids' building blocks in the sandpit. Kids love them, it's a great way to recycle and it's as cheap as chips.
Brenda Jarvis, South Yarra, Vic.

- If you need scrap material for quilts or to make dolls' clothes for your kids, go to the op shop. Op shop clothes are a lot cheaper, the money goes to charity and you get some great fabrics, prints and laces.
Marie Alexopoulos, Beverly Hills, NSW.

- When you need to borrow money, borrow from a pessimist. They won't expect it back.
Irene Brown, Caloundra, Qld.

KATHLEEN TRIES IT OUT!

WACKY BUT IT WORKS

Put candles through Life Saver lollies on birthday cakes. It stops wax from dripping onto the cake and holds the candles in place. Plus, it's a great decoration, too!

- To save money, cut a sponge in half. You can use one side to scrub items such as pet bowls and ashtrays and save the other half for regular dishes.
  Abigail Mayer, Canning Vale, WA.

- A fun gift idea that doesn't cost the earth is to tie some instant Scratchies to a small pot plant to create a money tree.
  Donna Lovell, Fyshwick, ACT.

- Instead of buying expensive flavoured bottle water, make your own using just a little real juice mixed with some water.
  Lucy Waters, Bega, NSW.

- After shopping, always put your spare coins into a jar. Then when you need some odd change, you'll have it.
  K. Turner, Pheasant Creek, Vic.

MONEY SAVING

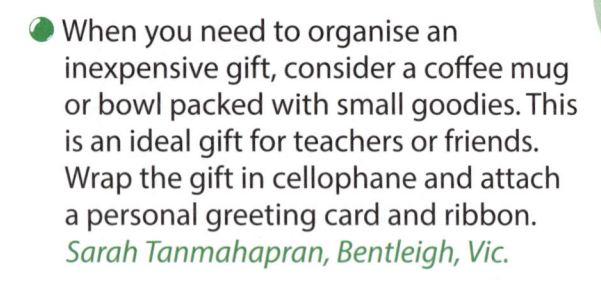

- When you need to organise an inexpensive gift, consider a coffee mug or bowl packed with small goodies. This is an ideal gift for teachers or friends. Wrap the gift in cellophane and attach a personal greeting card and ribbon.
Sarah Tanmahapran, Bentleigh, Vic.

- Wooden laundry pegs seal food in bags just as well as the plastic clips you can buy. They cost less, too.
Mary Maucher, Orelia, WA.

- To reduce the cost of filter fibre for fish tanks, use the wool stuffing from an old toy. It's cheaper but still an effective alternative.
Urszula Marciniak, Robina, Qld.

Keep your strawberry punnets to use for small seedlings or plants. They're ideal if you're giving seedlings to friends.
Michelle Grant, Collie, WA.

MONEY SAVING

164

- Save all your soap scraps till there's enough to fill a jar, then put them into a blender with a quarter of a cup of water and the juice of one lemon. Blend and put the liquid into a hand dispenser.
Marg Smith, Bundaberg, Qld.

- On someone's birthday, stick a picture or special photo on the front of a piece of cardboard. It creates a unique and personalised card and costs less, too!
Marilyn Cornish, Dee Why, NSW.

- One big way to save money is to drastically cut down on the amount of television you watch. You'll have less exposure to spending-inducing ads and a lower electricity bill.
Gregory Mills, Lamington, WA.

- Recycle old calendars by using them to make envelopes for birthday cards or wrapping presents.
Marianne McGowan, Epping, NSW.

- To save money and get squeaky clean windows, mix a weak solution of dishwashing liquid and water, then add a few drops of methylated spirits. To get a streak-free shine, polish with newspaper.
Melissa Anne, Mansfield, Qld.

- For a cheap pouch for your e-reader, use a micro-fibre mitt and sew in the sides to make it fit, then attach a loop and button.
Vivien Wakefield, Golden Beach, Qld.

- For instant mozzie repellent, fill a spray bottle with Listerine and spray it outdoors. It's great to use around the picnic table or barbecue area. It lasts a few days and is a cheap alternative to aerosol cans.
Michelle Cannon, Torrington, NSW.

- A great way to decorate your home without spending a lot of money is to buy inexpensive plastic containers or buckets and decorate them with stickers and beads. They can be used as storage bins to keep everything neat and tidy.
Jenna French, Mackay, Qld.

- Recycle old whiskey bottles by spraying them with black enamel and painting an outback pub scene on them. You can them use them for decoration around the house or even as a lamp base.
Lorene Bryant, Jamberoo, NSW.

- Don't toss out a shirt because of a broken button – sew on a new one. Don't toss out pants because of a hole in them – sew on a patch and save them for times when you're working around the house. This will save you money in the long run.
Karen Langlois, Brisbane, Qld.

- If you can't afford a GPS, don't panic – you can still avoid getting lost. Before you set off, write down each direction on a Post-it Note. Stick each note on your steering wheel, starting with the last direction at the bottom. As you drive along, you can peel off each one as you go. Cheap and easy.
Terry Farren, Kingsford, NSW.

- Inexpensive fleecy throw rugs make lovely warm ponchos. Just cut a hole in the centre big enough for your head to fit through bind the edges with tape and instantly you'll have a warm, versatile and affordable poncho.
Winifred Valdez, Canowie Belt, SA.

- Recycle used large spring-water containers into handy carry containers for gardening tools or household products. Simply cut out side panels leaving the centre support handle. Bind the handle with twine or rope to protect hand from any sharp edges.
Kellie Bush, Sutherland, NSW.

- If you are a one person household but love your pasta sauces, buy the largest jar you can and decant it into freezer safe containers for future use. I find two to three tablespoons is enough for one serving of pasta and there is no waste!
Maxine Wade, Neutral Bay, NSW.

- Drink a big glass of water before each meal in order to stay fuller longer and ultimately eat less. Not only will you save on the food bill, but you'll also feel better.
Tania Lords, Enfield, NSW.

- A great way to save money is to shop at the end of the day – bread, cakes, meats and other products cooked daily are often reduced in the evenings to clear stock.
Tina Richardson, South Perth, WA.

KATHLEEN TRIES IT OUT!

WACKY BUT IT WORKS

I keep change in a clear snap-lock bag so I can always see if I have enough coins for any little daily purchases like coffee. It also means I have a small emergency stash if my wallet is stolen.

MONEY SAVING

- A great way to save money on books is to buy them cheaply from op shops and return them when you've finished with them so they can resell them. You will be saving money and helping charity at the same time!
Sandra Knight, Westfield, WA.

- Mix together a jar of your favourite coffee and a jar of a non-branded version to make your coffee last twice as long. It tastes just as good and will save you money.
Jared Payne, Geelong, Vic.

- Garage sales are a great place to score awesome deals on items housewares, shoes, clothing, or even sports equipment.
Dorothy Lovatt, Padstow, NSW.

- If you want to jazz up your home entranceway but don't want to spend any money, pull apart a palette and rebuild it to fit your entranceway size, then nail wood panelling over the top, and stain. Slide it in and out when you want to restain it. Use whatever wood off-cut pieces that you can find and create your own unique entrance.
Suzanne Warmington, Lyons, ACT.

- The energy saved from recycling one aluminium can, can power a television set for three hours.
Nadine Hernandez, Carine, WA.

- Make your own inexpensive shower cleaner by diluting bleach in a spray bottle – spray your shower and leave for a few minutes before rinsing.
H. Wong, Clarkson, WA.

- Save on seedling trays by cutting empty toilet roll tubes in half, folding in base and filling with potting mix.
Amanda Piper, Hobart, Tas.

- It's easy to spend online when you have your card information stored in an account – just click and buy. Break this habit by never saving your card details.
Urszula Marciniak, Robina, Qld.

A great way to recycle old buckets is to make small holes in the bottom, fill with potting mix and use as a planter pot. They're cheap and look great.
Gwen Welch, Warwick, WA.

- I lowered the temperature gauge on my gas hot water system. And now because the water doesn't need to heat to the top temperature any more, I've reduced my quarterly gas bill.
G. Zimmermann, Norlane, Vic.

- We rarely ever buy bread at the store these days, mainly because the bread I make is not only cheaper, but tastier too.
H. Parkes, Noosa, Qld.

MONEY SAVING

169

🟡 My daughter and I enjoyed earth hour so much that we've made it a regular occurrence. One night a week we turn off the lights and TV and play cards surrounded by candlelight. We're saving money and power and have fun, too.
Charlie Mathis, Killara, NSW.

🟢 Make a list before you leave home to do the shopping. It sounds simple, but how many times have you wasted money by buying something you already have two of in the cupboard at home? Stick to your list and you won't go home with costly unwanted goods.
Rosanna Sosa, Port Adelaide, SA.

🟡 A wide-brimmed hat covered with a plastic bag does the job of an umbrella, but leaves both hands free, and is much cheaper.
Graham Morton, Beerwah, Qld.

🟢 Try to find another set of parents or two that you trust, and swap nights of babysitting with them. If you can pull it off, you'll get occasional evenings free without the cost of a babysitter and save a ton of money in the process.
Heather Warren, Wiley Park, NSW.

🟡 Save water while doing the dishes by washing up in the pot that you cooked dinner in – you'll use heaps less water.
Trish Baker, Darwin, NT.

- Cut holes in the bottom of an upside down ice-cream container for a makeshift toothbrush holder. It's cost-effective and keeps toothbrush heads from sitting in a pool of germy water.
Cassie Millar, Milsons Point, NSW.

- You can reuse your roll sunscreen by simply refilling the bottle from a bulk pack and popping the ball back in. It's very cost-effective during the summer.
Mary Kennedy, Redcliffe, Qld.

- The quickest and easiest way to double your money is to fold it over and put it back into your wallet.
Jim Deagn, Cairns, Qld.

- Use your dryer on medium, not high, to use less power.
Helen Khalid, Raymond Terrace, NSW.

- As I wait for the water to turn hot in the shower, I collect the cold water in a bucket then use it to water my plants or fill the dog's water bowl.
B. Urban, Eumundi, Qld.

- Buy washing powder in bulk. It works out to be so much cheaper.
Margaret Button, Penguin, Vic.

- Buy generic products. Dried and canned foods, such as pasta and tuna cost a fraction of branded goods and taste the same.
Leonie Myong, Fremantle, WA.

WACKY BUT IT WORKS

If I'm running low on cooking space in my kitchen, I open the top drawer and place the cutting board over it for extra room.

KATHLEEN TRIES IT OUT!

MONEY SAVING

12 TIPS FOR KEEPING ENERGY COSTS DOWN

- Dress for the temperature. Layering clothes and wearing wool helps keep you warm in winter, and means you can turn your heater down.
Olga Green, Sanctuary Point, NSW.

- Only heat or cool the rooms you spend the most time in to save on electricity and shut doors to the rooms you're not using.
Yolanda Faris, Glenelg, SA.

- You can save around $115 per year by washing clothes in cold water. You can also save by making sure you select the shortest appropriate washing cycle and waiting until you have a full load.
Neil Sosa, Townsville, Qld.

- Make sure your curtains or blinds seal your windows properly, and keep your curtains closed at night, and during the day when there is a heat-wave. Also try to block air coming in around doors and windows.
Helen Mayver, Christchurch, NZ.

- Use a power board, because it not only supplies electricity to multiple appliances at the same time, it also means you can switch off all appliances using the same switch.
Tim Kay, Burwood, NSW.

- When using the stove, keep lids on pots and saucepans when cooking to reduce the amount of time and energy used. Dinner will cook faster, too, so it's win-win.
Edith Brownleigh, St Kilda, Vic.

- To make sure your fridge is running efficiently, check that the door seal is tight and free from gaps so cold air can't escape. I was also told that an ideal fridge temperature is four or five degrees and an ideal freezer temperature is minus 15 to minus 18 degrees. If you have a second fridge, only turn it on when you need it.
Gary Jenkins, Sale, Vic.

- Did you know your phone charger is still using energy even when your phone isn't attached? Gadgets and appliances that are on standby still use energy so turn things off at the power point.
Patricia Weston, Perth, WA.

An insulated ceiling makes a big difference to your energy bills. If you already have insulation installed, check that it is has the right rating.
Trinity Downs, Narooma, NSW.

- Thaw frozen food in your fridge or on the bench, instead of the microwave, to reduce cooking time and energy used.
Harriet Pappas, South Melbourne, Vic.

- Use the water-saving cycle on your dishwasher and only put it on when it's full.
Jane Harris, Camden, NSW.

- Replace old incandescent and halogen light globes with energy-efficient globes. Energy-efficient globes save power and last longer.
Danielle Sheridan, Mackay, Qld.

PETS

174

PETS

PETS

🟢 Buy toothpaste suitable for dogs. Human toothpaste is made to spit out and your dog is going to swallow it, regardless.
Katherine Sio, Canley Vale, NSW.

🔴 Sticky tape a piece of ribbon to a table and you have an instant, simple but fun toy for your cat!
Lucy Kliem, Berowra Heights, NSW.

🟢 Before you brush your dog's teeth, dip the toothbrush in a mixture of water and garlic salt and let your dog lick the brush so it knows the taste is good.
Michelle Tomkins, Hervey Bay, Qld.

🔴 Cats scratch to mark their territory, for exercise and for pure pleasure – and it's going to be hard for you to stop them doing it. You can, however, direct them to where you want them to scratch. Invest in a scratching post and place it near the furniture she's been adding her own personal decoration to. Feed her or play with her near the post to encourage her interest in it.
Reannen Jones, Georges Hall, NSW.

🟢 Instead of throwing away your old pillow, turn it into a new bed for your furry friend.
Sarah Wright, Wakeley, NSW.

KATHLEEN TRIES IT OUT!

WACKY BUT IT WORKS

When I notice a hole in the wall, I don't buy expensive wall plaster. The kids' playdough does the same thing and can be made with ingredients you'll already have at home!

- If travelling on road trips with your dog, a harness is a great option. It provides your dog some freedom, but restrains them in case of an accident. Be sure to buy a harness that's specifically designed to be used with safety seatbelts.
Joan Garth, Mollymook, NSW.

- Research what health issues your pet may face so you're aware of the early signs. Cats, for example, are prone to kidney failure and diabetes later in life, and early detection is vital.
Ingrid Luell, Mooloolaba, Qld.

- On a hot day, freeze half low-salt stock and half water in a plastic cup, and put a rawhide twist in it. It is a great summer treat for your dog.
M. Dominick, Narromine, NSW.

- Pick a routine and stick to it. Animals dislike disruption as much as we do. It can cause anxiety, which can in turn lead to behavioural issues.
Yvette Thomas, Shepparton, Vic.

● When brushing your dog's teeth, only brush the outside of the teeth, the tongue will take care of the inside.
Janice Forsham, Miama, Qld.

● With any big changes, such as a new addition to your family or a house move, keep your pet involved so they don't feel neglected. Introduce them to their new surroundings or person in an exciting happy way so they know the change is a good thing for them, too.
Diane Curtin, Cabramatta, NSW.

● Pets with fair skin can get sunburnt, too. Apply zinc cream to sensitive areas to prevent your pet from getting skin cancer.
Jules Bailey, Moe, Vic.

● To keep kitty litter smelling fresh, sprinkle a little talcum powder in the bottom of the tray.
C. Bebb, Kenwick, WA.

PETS

- If you have pets, keep your home smelling fresh with perfumed pouches attached to a fan. It's an inexpensive way to freshen a room.
Jacqui Dutton, Port Kennedy, WA.

- To remove pet hair, put on a pair of rubber gloves and dampen hands with water, then rub on clothes and furniture to remove hair.
Lyn Goodwin, Forbes, NSW.

- To remove the smell of cat urine, scrub the affected area with eucalyptus oil mixed with water. Cats dislike the smell of eucalyptus so this also acts as a deterrent to prevent re-offending.
Poppy Haydon, Rochedale South, Qld.

- To stop ants getting into your pet's bowl of food, simply place a dinner plate underneath, filled with water, so the ants can't reach it.
Peta Spence, Avoca Beach, NSW.

- If your pet is scared of storms, help them get over their fear by playing a CD of storms while you're home, very low at first and gradually increasing in sound over time. If your dog is afraid, don't attend to the fearful behaviour. Redirect him to a fun activity, like playing ball.
Natalie Barber, Dorset Vale, SA.

- A treat for a teething puppy is chewing on frozen ice cubes of stock. It'll soothe their teeth and gums.
Kellie Peterson, Mandurah, WA.

- Take a shower cap with you whenever you take your dog for a walk. You can fill it up at any tap and satisfy your thirsty dog. A great portable water dish.
Angelina Reeves, Heathcote, Vic.

● If you often travel with your dog or cat, it's handy to keep a lint roller in your glove box so you can arrive at your destination without annoying pet hair all over your clothes.
Trudi Thomas, Glenelg, SA.

● An inexpensive way to keep your cat entertained is to cut rings out of toilet paper rolls – they'll love throwing them around.
Lucy Poppet, Hobart, Tas.

● When walking our dogs at night, we put glow sticks around their necks so drivers can see them.
Eugene Garcia, Greystanes, NSW.

● To stop your puppy chewing on the wooden furniture, wipe a small amount of oil of cloves over it.
Molly Sutton, Coorparoo, Qld.

● If your pet has a bandaged paw, rub the outside of the bandage with soap to stop them chewing on it. They hate the taste.
James Henderson, Alderley, Qld.

● A simple way to crush a tablet for your pet is to use a garlic crusher. It breaks it into tiny pieces you can than add to food.
Danielle Hays, Wodonga, Vic.

KATHLEEN TRIES IT OUT!

WACKY BUT IT WORKS

You can make this flashy fan, just by gluing old CDs together. It will keep you cool during the year-round Australian heat.

- Don't throw out old pillows, just cover them with two pillow cases, and place them in your dog's kennel. They'll appreciate the soft bedding.
  Alyssa Peters, Palm Cove, Qld.

- To make a dry wash for your dog, combine 2 cups of cornflour (to absorb oil), ½ cup of baking soda (to deodorise) and ½ cup of salt (to loosen dirt). Massage the powder into your dog's fur and leave for five minutes before brushing the powder out.
  Robyn Whitehead, Springwood, Qld.

WACKY BUT IT WORKS

🟢 I've found a quirky way to recycle my old gumboots rather than simply throwing them out – by planting seedlings inside the legs! Visitors to my garden always comment on my unique flowering 'pots'.
Jean Lawrence, Sheffield, Tas.

🟠 My husband was petrified of spiders so I kept putting them in unexpected places until he saw the funny side and wasn't scared.
D. Canter, Lonsdale, SA.

🟢 Place a mouse trap on the top of your alarm clock to stop from hitting the snooze button in the morning!
Emma Brown, Albury, Vic.

🟠 Unwanted bras stretched between tree branches make perfect feeding stations for birds.
Kelly McAndrew, Auckland, NZ.

🟢 When it starts to get colder outside, hard boil a couple of eggs and pop them into your pockets before leaving the house. They stay hot for ages and keep your hands warm. When they cool down, you can eat them as a healthy snack.
Pip Monroe, Yarraville, Vic.

KATHLEEN TRIES IT OUT!

182

- To prevent your snorkel or goggles from fogging, spread a little toothpaste on the inside of the mask before diving into the water.
Lynette Binder, Earlville, Qld.

- If the plug of your rubber thong pulls out, push it back through the hole and fix a bread clip underneath it to stop it happening again.
Sherry Black, Nundah, Qld.

- I take a homemade salad to work for lunch each day, with an olive oil and balsamic vinegar dressing. At first I wasn't sure how to transport the dressing without it leaking in my bag. Then I found the perfect solution... a urine sample container, which costs one dollar from the chemist. The seal is perfect. The only problem is explaining to your colleagues what you are pouring on your salad.
Lenita Grey, Cremorne, NSW.

- My children were impossible to get out of bed in the mornings until I bought a clown costume and did card tricks at the breakfast table. Now they're up before me.
Beverley Smith, Dee Why, NSW.

- If you love playing music on your phone put it in an empty glass – it works like a speaker and makes the music so much louder!
Nancy Wong, Belconnen, ACT.

OFFICE/GIFTS/CRAFT

OFFICE /GIFTS /CRAFT

OFFICE / GIFTS / CRAFT

● Place sticky tape rolls in the fridge for about an hour before you use them to avoid the tape splitting and breaking.
Narelle Dobson, Geelong, Vic.

● Buy some small boxes, and throughout the year, buy toiletries when they're on special. Fill the boxes with these and finish with artificial flowers, ribbon and so on. They are perfect to take to people in hospital.
Brenda Ruthers, Ipswich, Qld.

● When visiting a loved one in a nursing home, take along some photo albums or past holiday snaps. They will love them and will help jog their long-term memory.
Flora Morales, Bowral, NSW.

Run the sticky edge of a Post-it note over and between your keyboard keys. It will pick up all the dust and dirt.
Cora Neeson, Woolloomooloo, NSW.

● When taking group photos, have the person with the camera count to three and instruct people to blink on two. This will avoid closed eyes in the photo.
Danielle Harris, Essendon, Vic.

● I don't throw out flowers that I receive as a gift; I dry them out and cut them up to make potpourri. Then the lovely gift lasts for much longer.
Skye Silas, Parramatta, NSW.

KATHLEEN TRIES IT OUT!

WACKY BUT IT WORKS

No need to buy a proper piping set if you're just making cupcakes for family and friends – cut a small hole in the corner of a zip-lock bag and use that instead.

- A great use for old X-rays is to use them as template for sewing and craftwork. They keep their shape well and don't tear or bend.
Anita Beck, Mt Lawley, WA.

- To store rolls of wrapping paper, simply cut off a leg from a pair of old pantihose and place them in that. The nylon stretches and allows a lot of rolls to be stored together and you can easily see which one you want.
Dianne Adams, Chadstone, Vic.

- Refrigerate birthday candles the day before lighting them and you'll find you won't end up with messy drops of wax over the cake.
Steven Taunton, Killara, NSW.

OFFICE/GIFTS/CRAFT

187

- Use a paper towel holder to keep your spools of ribbon organised and easy to get to.
Zanisha Ali, Palmerston North, Qld.

- Use a stubby holder to hold and protect your portable hard drive – it's the perfect size and the material is waterproof and flexible.
Bonnie Hayes, Balcatta, WA.

- When giving a birthday card in person, don't write anything on the envelope so the person you're giving it to can reuse it later.
Shelley Sprague, Lindfield, NSW.

- To preserve expensive marker pens, store them in a sealed soft drink bottle. This stops them from drying out and they last longer.
John O'Shea, Revesby, NSW.

- Use a rubber band as a bookmark – it won't fall out if you're carrying it in a bag and it won't mark the pages.
Dave Mason, Wodonga, Vic.

- Instead of sending out boring paper invitations, why not try attaching your invite to sweets or chocolate bars. Your guests will love the thoughtful and unique gesture.
Robyn Silcox, Bundaberg, Qld.

- To prevent any ink stains and make it easier to find my pen in my handbag I carry my pen in a toothbrush holder.
Mavis Penfold, Nurwee, NSW.

- Old tubes of superglue can harden over time, even with the cap on. Prevent this by keeping them in the fridge. They'll last forever.
Noel Markus, Hobart, Tas.

- To extend the life of dried out felt pens, dip them in a saucer of white vinegar, leave for about 15 seconds, dab with paper towel and then they're ready to go again.
Larissa Yu, Tempe, NSW.

- If you have brooches that you don't wear anymore, glue a magnet on the back – they make great fridge magnets, and you're recycling at the same time.
Janice Anderson, Toorak, Vic.

- Did you know you can de-mist the glass of your watch by turning it over and wearing the front against your skin.
Narelle Collison, Blacktown, NSW.

- Keep a container filled with labelled barcodes and product details, that way, when entering competitions it's easy to get the details you need.
Amanda Simpson, Nowra, NSW.

OFFICE/GIFTS/CRAFT

● Use a dry bar of soap as a pin cushion. Needles and pins will slide easily through any type of material – and smell nice, too.
Sam Nicholson, Yanchep, WA.

● Instead of keeping all your recipes in a folder, why not use your smartphone to take a photo of them. Not only will they take up less space, but you'll always have the recipe with you when shopping for ingredients.
Michelle Di Micco, Gorokan, NSW.

● Keep a large-sized zip-lock bag in your handbag – it's ideal to slip your wet fold-up umbrella in until you get home.
Stephanie Clarke, Toowoomba, Qld.

● Vintage sewing patterns and even old wallpaper are a quirky way to wrap up presents.
Jane Lawrence, Sheffield, Tas.

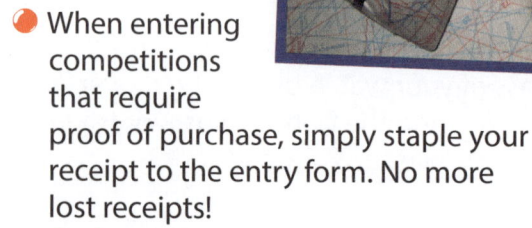

● When entering competitions that require proof of purchase, simply staple your receipt to the entry form. No more lost receipts!
Carlea Visco, Deception Bay, Qld.

KATHLEEN TRIES IT OUT!

WACKY BUT IT WORKS

If you find there's too much icing on a cupcake, even it out, by cutting it in half and placing the bottom half on the top, so that the icing is now in the middle.

- Reuse baby formula tins by spray-painting and labelling them. They look terrific, and they're great for storing craft items.
Kerri Powell, Narellan Vale, NSW.

- If you have a metal zip that sticks, rub a lead pencil along it.
C. Bebb, Kenwick, WA.

- Place your laptop on top of empty egg cartons to keep it from overheating.
K. Simpson, Carlton, Vic.

- If you find buying presents for elderly relatives hard, why not make them a special memory board? Simply pin photos of their family, pets, friends, and so on to a corkboard. It means so much more than a box of chocolates.
Donna Rogers, St Kilda, Vic.

OFFICE/GIFTS/CRAFT

- To gift wrap bottles of wine, use the netting from tomatoes or oranges and tie at the neck with a ribbon.
Franca Wigg, Seaton, SA.

- Keep your Take 5 mag beside the phone for when you're put on hold. You can do the puzzles while you wait… and wait…
Brent Reed, Rokeby, Tas.

- Save empty Tic Tac boxes – they're the ideal size for storing small spools of ribbons.
Fatima Kheller, Albury, NSW.

- When putting photos into albums, stop them from buckling by inserting a ruler between the sleeves and simply sliding the picture along the ruler.
Stacey Rams, Salisbury Plains, SA.

- When you buy a new flat-screen TV, always keep the original box, so that if and when you move house you can pack it carefully.
Alicia Kinsey, Pymble, NSW.

Keep a small bulldog clip on your key ring that holds your list of things to do when you're out. It's always with you so there are no excuses for leaving your list at home or forgetting anything.
Kelly Punter, Perth, WA.

- When knitting, use dark needles when making something with light wool and light needles when using dark wool. It makes it much easier to see when counting stitches.
W. Fletcher, Craigie, WA.

- Keep a pen in your reading-glasses case, so you always have one handy when you need it for puzzles or paperwork.
Elspeth Lovell, Leslie Vale, Tas.

- Create a colourful inspiration board by cutting out the Wise Words from old Take 5 magazines and pinning them to a corkboard.
Dana Murden, Atherton, Qld.

- Wrapping paper makes terrific wall art. Simply cut to size and frame it behind glass, then hang it up. It's a cheap and fun way to brighten up a room.
Mel Hoye, Kariong, NSW.

- Use magnetic strips to store things like bobby pins and tweezers.
Bel Tcaciuc, Amphitheatre, Vic.

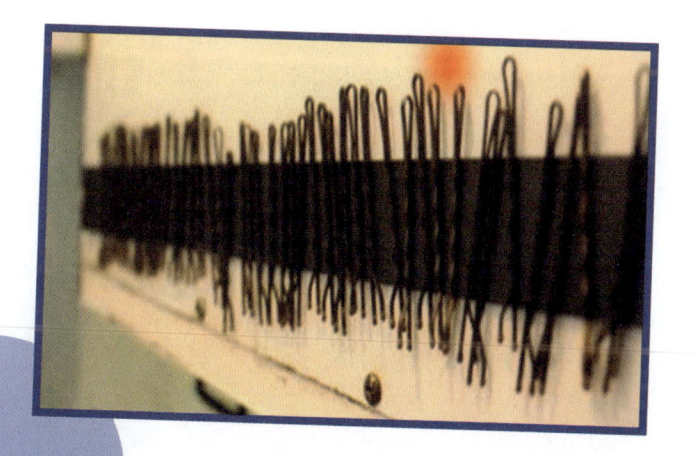

OFFICE/GIFTS/CRAFT

- When assembling build-it-yourself furniture, use a muffin tray to separate the different nails and screws. The small compartments are perfect for all the tiny parts.
Shaun Cowdell, via email.

- To help me quickly locate the right shade of thread for my sewing project, I store similar-coloured thread together in zip-lock bags.
Cathy Agius, Homebush, NSW.

- Every time you go shopping, keep an eye out for gifts for friends and family. Buying gifts throughout the year will save a lot of stress when birthdays and Christmas rolls around.
Hannah Evans, Lismore, NSW.

- To keep new sticky tape rolls handy for use, just thread them onto an old dog collar or belt and hang them on a hook.
Jeannette Gilbert, Rosebery, NSW.

- For a cute and unique way to wrap your presents, try crocheting some lace strips and use with brown paper. Easy, special and colourful!
Lucy Kliem, Long Jetty, NSW.

- To prevent the cards in your purse sticking together, wrap a piece of ribbon around each and tie the ends. They will slip out easily when you pull on the ends of the ribbon.
Kelly Bundock, Neutral Bay, NSW.

- Save the zipped or buttoned plastic bags that new linen comes in to reuse for other items. They make great toiletries, first-aid, craft and baby travel bags, and you can easily see what you are looking for at a quick glance.
Kylee Southon, Waikanae, NZ.

- If you don't have time for exercise, try multi-tasking. Do sit-ups in TV ad breaks and squats while brushing your teeth.
Catherine Lillington, Wynnum, Qld.

- Highlight your receipts with a highlighter to stop fading – it's very helpful for tax time.
Celia Cameron, Coolum, Qld.

- Save all your treasured photos in an emergency by scanning them onto a USB that's easy to grab in a hurry.
Gwenda Plumridge, Castlemaine, Vic.

- If you run out of gift wrap, use aluminium foil instead. Adding a ribbon makes the gift look complete.
Helen Robinson, Helensvale, Qld.

WACKY BUT IT WORKS

Most people forget that a dishwasher can be used to wash more than just dirty dishes. I throw everything from my kids' plastic toys to their shoes, hats and hairbrushes in. My hubby even washes his tools and hubcaps in it.
Polly Ellis, Ballarat, Vic.

- If you've got a lot of cards to post, wet a sponge and wipe it across the backs of the stamps. It saves getting the nasty taste in your mouth.
I. Bagnall, Morningside, Qld.

- To keep track of your internet passwords, keep a diary next to your computer and write down your login details and passwords.
Angela Sikiric, Cronulla, NSW.

- If you update your camera, keep the old one in your car's glovebox. If you're involved in a car accident or road incident, you can take photos of any damage, number plates and the scene of the incident, on the spot.
Steven Taunton, Killara, NSW.

- To efficiently wrap gifts and avoid wrinkled paper, make sure you lay the present and paper on a hard surface to start.
Jane Young, Brunswick, Vic.

- Reuse plastic bags that newspapers are delivered in. They're very strong, and ideal for covering wet umbrellas to carry in your handbag.
Corinne Hall, Golden Grove, SA.

- To tie a parcel securely, first wet the string. As it dries, the string will shrink and leave the parcel sealed securely.
Peta Suarez, Casula, NSW.

- Tackle boxes are great to store all of your craft and sewing accessories.
Kylie Turner, Bundaberg, Qld.

- Forget boring thank you cards... I like to give my family and friends a pretty personalised pebble instead! You can paint their name on it and they can keep it forever. You have to hand deliver it though, because they're too heavy to post.
Dolores Carter, Lewisham, NSW.

KIDS

198

KIDS

199

KIDS

● After washing your children's bath toys, hang them out to dry in an onion bag on the washing line.
Rita McDonald, Red Cliffs, Vic.

● Try adding a few dots of fabric paint to the bottom of your kids' socks to add grip and stop them slipping over.
Virginia Montgomery, Colac, Vic.

● My kids love to use glitter in their artworks, but it's really annoying to clean up. Luckily I've found that using a lint roller gets all of it off the table quickly and easily.
Margaret Collins, Wattle Grove, NSW.

● Kids' paints can be expensive so make your own by dissolving ½ cup flour in a pan with one cup water. Add three cups boiling water and boil for one minute until it thickens. Allow to cool, then divide into portions and stir one to two teaspoons of non-toxic powder paint into each one.
Lisa Travis, Perth, WA.

● Even though most cleaning products have child-proof lids these days, I also like to tie a little bell to the top of mine to alert me if my little ones are trying to get their hands on them.
Andréa Nutt, Dianella, WA.

KATHLEEN TRIES IT OUT!

WACKY BUT IT WORKS

Paper snowflakes are so easy and cheap to make but absolutely beautiful decorations for Christmas or festive occasions. Just grab some paper, fold it in half, and cut little shapes into it.

- If your child loves putting nappies on their dolls, cut old towels into triangles and attach buttons. This is cheaper than buying store-bought nappies.
Maria Pagonis, Caboolture, Qld.

- My granddaughter has recently started crawling so my daughter used her old blow-up pool to create a safe play area for her. It's big enough for her to crawl around as much as she likes and the walls are cushioned so she can't hurt herself.
Joyce Chin, Deniliquin, NSW.

- Add a drop of food colouring to ice cubes before freezing them. It's a fun way to encourage your kids to drink more water.
Clayton Gardner, Elizabeth Bay, NSW.

KIDS

- A cheap and easy way to keep young children entertained over the holidays is by playing a supermarket game. Rather than spend money on toy food, I save all my empty food containers like salt, pepper, sugar and herbs. They love playing with them and it doesn't cost anything extra.
Julie Walker, Penguin, Tas.

- Use a hanging rack to store cleaning products. This keeps them nicely organised and away from the kids.
Iona Samson, Maroubra, NSW.

- When my kids want to play outside on sunny days, I peg a dark sheet over the clothesline. They play happily in the shade for ages.
Edwin Cole, Rose Bay, NSW.

- If your child is learning to stay dry at night, use puppy training mats in their bed to soak up any accidents. Then you just remove the mat and the bed is still dry!
Tamina Goodchild, Modbury, SA.

- We all remember sun block for our kids but it's important to protect their eyes with sunglasses, too.
Dee Yearling, Williamtown, Vic.

- Remember to turn off or remove batteries from toys. Batteries will last longer and the toys won't be damaged if batteries corrode.
Lucinda Clarkson, Werribee, Vic.

- If you have young kids, don't throw away the coloured caps on cordial bottles. Use them to teach kids to count and to learn colours.
Wendy Khoury, Noosa, Qld.

- Set up a photo booth at a kids' birthday party. Buy some costume accessories from a $2 shop and you're away – the kids will love it and you'll have plenty of snaps from the day.
Charlize Hopkins, Long Jetty, NSW.

- If the kids have accidentally (or not so accidentally!) drawn all over their desk with pen, spray the area with hairspray, then simply wipe the mark away.
Paige Rogers, Mount Gambier, SA.

- If you've bought the kids a new board game for Christmas, it's a good idea to cover the board with some clear contact. It helps preserve the surface and if something gets spilt on it you can easily wipe it clean.
Narelle Smith, Harris Park, NSW.

- When sending birthday cards to children, include flat chocolates instead of money as cash occasionally gets stolen. It doesn't matter if the chocolate melts slightly, it's still yummy.
Sarah Herbert, Bomaderry, NSW.

KIDS

203

● Make your own confetti with a hole punch and some used coloured wrapping paper or old envelopes. Get the kids to help; it's lots of fun.
Kathryn Parker, Seville East, Vic.

● My baby loves to roll around on the floor with no nappy but her 'little accidents' were ruining the carpet. A handy idea I discovered is to use a picnic blanket. The protective backing protects the carpet and I just pop it in the wash if it does get wet.
Kellie Levin, via email.

● Make inexpensive homemade magnets for the kids by cutting out pictures from the magazines and gluing them onto small squares of those soft plastic fridge magnets that often arrive as junk mail.
Debra Ellerson, Labrador, Qld.

● I have trouble cleaning inside my baby's bottle but discovered that a cotton bud works a treat, getting right up into the little crevices and leaving it nice and clean.
Julie Walker, North Strathfield, NSW.

● To create a cheap and easy child-safe lock for kitchen cupboards push a wooden spoon through the handles and secure with a rubber band.
Kelly Walker, Airport West, Vic.

KATHLEEN TRIES IT OUT!

WACKY BUT IT WORKS

If you want a summer glow without splashing out on expensive bronzer, just dab your make-up brush into some hot chocolate powder and sweep it over your cheeks. It will give you the same glow. Just don't be tempted to lick your face…

- To keep an easily distracted toddler in a pram while walking, try to play a fun game of spotting and counting things like finding 10 red cars, etc. It will keep them occupied and helps develop counting and observation skills, too.
Alana Everard, Clarinda, Vic.

- When preparing goodie bags for a kids' party, balance a broom stick between two objects and hang the loops of the bags along the stick. Then fill all at once.
Ellen Axford, Mt Gravatt, Qld.

- To help kids dish up their own cereal, divide the cereal into zip-lock bags. The bags are easier for the kids to pour from and there's less mess.
Angel Caplin, North Booval, Qld.

KIDS

205

- Encourage kids to be more active by playing I-spy while walking around the block.
K. Lowe, Yass, NSW.

- I read that some babies sleep better with their parents' scent near them so I put our baby's cot sheet in our bed for a couple of days, then put it on his cot. Now he sleeps soundly.
Ginger Duncan, Bowral, NSW.

- An easy way to get chewing gum out of a child's hair – without tears – is to spray WD40 on the gum. It will comb right out. But make sure you do it in a well-ventilated area.
Harriet Stretson, Mildura, SA.

- Personalise a recipe folder for your children when they move out of home by filling it with recipes they love and separating the sections with coloured dividers. It's a great moving out present and you'll know their eating well.
Yvonne Herrera, Beerwah, Qld.

- Set up a scavenger hunt in your backyard with clues and prizes to keep kids busy over the school holidays. Not only will it help kids develop reasoning skills but it will also encourage them to play outside and work in teams with their friends.
Fiona Harris, Cue, WA.

- To keep my daughter entertained, I let her paint her own artworks. The canvases can be bought cheaply from discount shops and they make great presents for family.
Kathy Sherman, Currimundi, Qld.

- Don't throw out big boxes if you have kids, save them up for a rainy day and then make 'racing cars'.
Danielle Coates, Lyons, ACT.

- Ever been caught out at a cafe without a bib? I ordered a messy chocolate sundae for my little one and created a bib out of a sheet of newspaper. No mess, no fuss and no expense!
Caroline Brown, Mortdale, NSW.

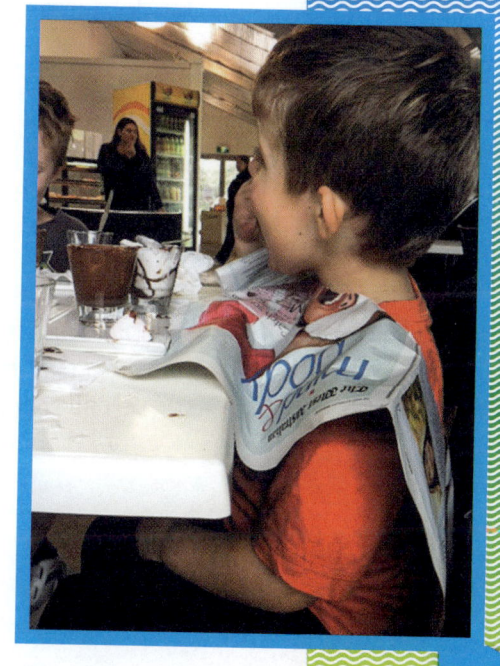

- My daughter loves lucky dips so I set up one at home. I spent $10 on a variety of toys, books and gifts from a discount store and wrapped them up in pretty paper. When she's good she gets to pick one out.
Luke Carpenter, Elizabeth, SA.

- My kids were always losing their good drink bottles on excursions, so now I save small plastic bottles for these trips. They can be filled with water, then put in the bin when the kids have finished with them. I've saved a lot of money this way.
Franklin Logan, Bull Creek, WA.

- When parents drop off children at your kid's party, be sure you know about any food allergies.
Romina Surrey, Mosman, NSW.

- To prepare my son for the first day of kindergarten, we did a dry run to ease his nerves. I organised a 'school day' where we got up in the morning, put on his uniform, packed his bag and walked to the school gate. It really helped him for when the real day came around.
Marie Oliver, Toowoomba, Qld.

- Use an air mattress pump to quickly blow u[p balloons for a party. Then you aren't left with that icky balloon taste in your mouth all day.
Rachael Williams, South Yarra, Vic.

- To encourage children to recycle, cover a cardboard box with cheap wrapping paper and let them cut out pictures of items that can be placed in the recycling bin – no more sorting through the rubbish on collection day.
Earnest Porter, Mount Gambier, SA.

- Use a hanging shoe rack in the pantry to organise your kids' snacks.
Sandra Tompson, Adelaide, SA.

WACKY BUT IT WORKS

If you need to get your hair out of your face, but don't have a hair tie handy, use a bulldog clip to keep it in place.
Skylar Simpson, Geraldton, WA.

- I find storing toy figurines in cupcake holders an easy and economical way to keep the toys together.
Sue Williams, Narre Warren South, Vic.

- To help everyone remember food allergies, I've written exactly what food is not allowed and placed it on the fridge, inside the cupboard and near the dining table. This can help remind dads, grandparents, babysitters and give you some peace of mind.
Lucy Kliem, Berowra Heights, NSW.

- Keep your cupboards stocked with healthy snacks for kids such as fruit, air-popped popcorn, unsalted nuts and yoghurt. Then there's no temptation to eat junk.
  Anita-Marie Sullivan, Mona Vale, NSW.

- A lettered pencil case is great for storing kid's paintbrushes. Use the letters enclosed to identify what's inside. It saves time looking for brushes when the kids are eager to start painting.
  Bobbie Burke, Fernvale, Qld.

- Avoid the struggle of getting kids to eat fruit and vegies by making pictures – like faces and animals – out of them.
  Maria Allen, North Ryde, NSW.

- To get my kids away from the TV screen and up and active, I set up an obstacle course in the backyard. It usually involves plants they have to jump over and chair tunnels to crawl through. They love it.
  Brent Porter, Huntfield Heights, SA.

- When taking children to crowded placed, write your mobile number on their arm. If you are separated, they'll be able to contact you easily.
Amanda Jennings, Parramatta, NSW.

- Egg cups make great sized containers for your kids gluing crafts or painting projects – small enough so if they spill it, it doesn't go everywhere.
Suzanne Warmington, Port Macquarie, NSW.

- Make your own muffins and cakes, packed full of fruit and vegies, including sultanas, carrot, zucchini, banana or pumpkin – the kids won't even know they're there.
Lorna Pippin, Padstow, NSW.

- Growing vegies and herbs at home can be a fun way to teach kids where food comes from and to encourage them to eat more greens.
Kathy Rutherford, Rosanna, Vic.

- Tablets can be really tough for kids to swallow but I find if you place it in a spoonful of yoghurt it usually slides down easily.
Georgia Sulley, Sandy Bay, Tas.

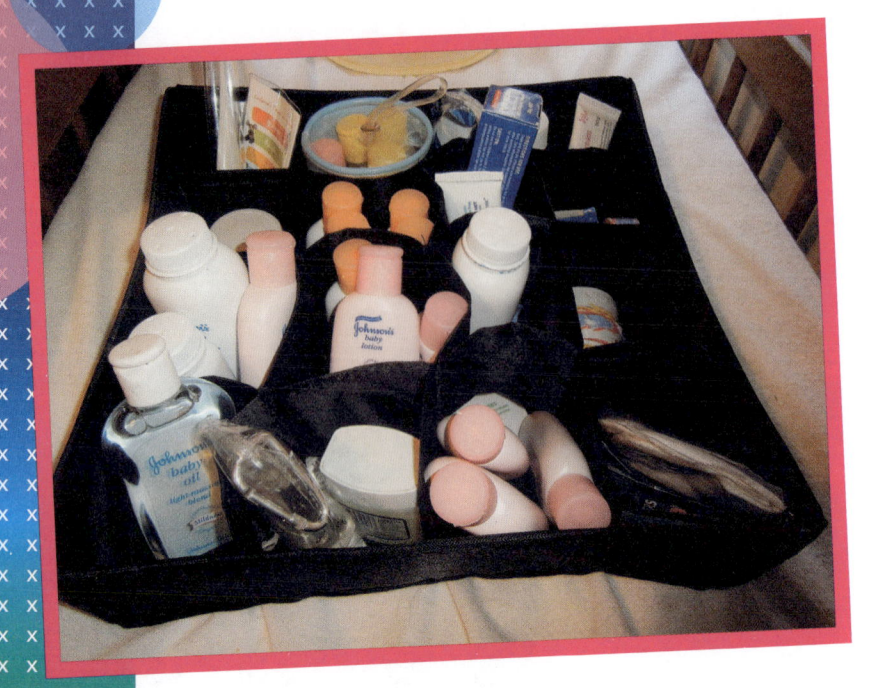

- Use a drawer divider insert to organise baby ointments, lotions and creams.
Stefanie Hinkley, Morphett Vale, SA.

- A fun and inexpensive way to keep the kids entertained is by giving them some coloured rice to play with, as an alternative to sand. Just add some food colouring to warm water and add the rice, then drain and leave the rice to dry outside. The more colours you make, the more fun they'll have.
Deena Clark, Epping, NSW.

- Try sticking bright and colourful number wall stickers on the back of the bathroom door to help your child with toilet training. It encourages them to stay there for longer, and helps them learn to count.
Kylie Davey, Drouin, Vic.

WACKY BUT IT WORKS

- Recycled Pringle containers are great for kids colouring pencils.
  Shirley Mires, Glebe, NSW.

- Buy cheap disposable change mats to use when your baby's cloth change mats are in the wash. As they're quite big, you can cut them into quarters and they cover the 'messy' area perfectly.
  Linda Buchanan, Mount Barker, SA.

- For a cheap DIY chalkboard, paint an old coffee table with chalkboard paint. The kids will be entertained for hours.
  Janice Saunders, Ashbury, NSW.

- Kids are more likely to become adventurous eaters if they know how to cook. Make it fun by giving them their own aprons and letting them help you regularly with small tasks.
  Linda Jacobs, Glenroy, Vic.

> I use leftover egg cartons instead of ice cube trays. They look better, the ice is bigger and you have enough room to freeze some fruit in the middle.
> *Sara Lowe, Moana, SA.*

> **I give my six-year-old daughter ice and have her suck it for a bit before giving her medicine – it numbs the tastebuds.**
> **Tyler Smith, Casuarina, NT.**

- When our son became more mobile, we used some of his old plastic chain link toys as child locks for our cupboards. They're cheaper and easier to use than most other child locks but they work perfectly.
  Lisa Bridges, Canterbury, NSW.

KIDS

213

Make baby's mealtimes quick and easy by pureeing food and freezing it in ice-cube trays. Store cubes in labelled zip-lock bags. Pop a cube or two in the microwave at dinner time and it's ready in a flash.
Kerry Price, Mansfield, Qld.

● Keep young children occupied when grocery shopping by cutting out a variety of pictures of grocery items and getting them to look for each item to be ticked off their list.
Anita Felmingham, Upper Freestone, Qld.

● Don't throw away the box your new TV comes in – make it into a cubbyhouse for the grandkids. I did and they really love it.
Fredrick Flowers, Mt Lawley, WA.

- Have your child pretend to give a stuffed animal medicine before she takes hers. It works for my little one.
Alix Davis, Brisbane, Qld.

- Use an empty wine bottle carton with partitions to make an inexpensive and fun toy car garage.
Anna Rochford, Erina, NSW.

- If your little one wakes up too early each day, put a clock in their room and let them know they can't get up to an agreed upon time. My son thinks this is a great game, plus it's teaching him to read time.
Susan Piper, Bankstown, NSW.

Pour softened ice-cream into a cake pan, then decorate with whipped cream and lollies for a quick kids' ice-cream cake.
Maureen Stern, Rosedale, Vic.

- Pikelets don't have to be boring. While making some for my hungry grandchildren we added a few chocolate sprinkles to the mixture.
C. Fair, Mornington, Tas.

- Eyedrops are hard to give, especially when little ones are flinching and squirming. Try holding the bottle in your hands for two to three minutes to warm it to body temperature. Sometimes cool drops don't feel good.
Pat Thorn, Milperra, NSW.

- Use the trays from a box of chocolates to make quirky shaped ice cubes. It's always a hit with the kids!
M. Buckley, Noble Park, Vic.

- It's worth forking out money on labels for kids' school items. When the kids lose things they can be easily returned and it'll end up being cheaper than replacing lost items.
Taylah Rickards, Hobart, Tas.

● Stuff a miniature marshmallow in the bottom of an ice-cream cone. This will help to prevent kids getting messy from ice-cream dripping out and they get an extra tasty treat at the end.
Sonja Shaw, Cronulla, NSW.

● I always keep a bottle opener in my car for when my daughter wants a bottled drink while we're out and about. I simply make a hole in the lid with the point of the bottle opener and poke a straw through it – no more spills and everyone's happy.
Priscilla Watkins, via email.

● Tiny Barbie shoes really hurt when you step on them. If these little accessories are left all over your house, buy a box designed to hold screws or nails. They fit perfectly.
Lucy Chelmsford, Darwin, NT.

10 TIPS FOR PACKING KIDS' LUNCH BOXES

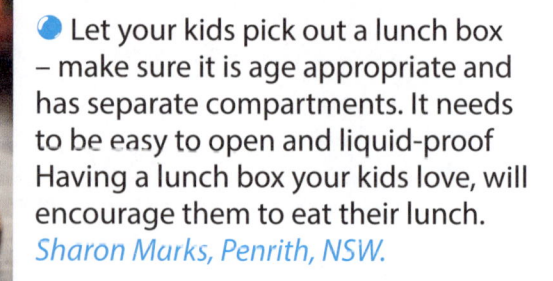

🔵 Let your kids pick out a lunch box – make sure it is age appropriate and has separate compartments. It needs to be easy to open and liquid-proof Having a lunch box your kids love, will encourage them to eat their lunch.
Sharon Marks, Penrith, NSW.

🔴 Make sure there is always room to keep your kids' lunch box chilled with an ice brick or frozen drink bottle. This will keep food fresh and crisp.
Lana Stevenson, Bringelly, NSW.

🔵 Start with a plan for the week and get the kids to help. I write a list and take the kids shopping with me, then we spend Sunday preparing their food for the week. This has made them more interested in food and healthy choices.
Janice Feung, Labrador, Qld.

🔴 Make a little extra at dinner time each night and then you can pack the leftovers into lunch boxes. This saves time and money.
Kay Thomas, Port Adelaide, SA.

🔵 Freezing fruit like orange segments and grapes is a great way to keep kids hydrated. They will especially love it in summer.
Larissa Donovan, Port Fairy, Vic.

- Get creative! If you have fussy eaters, why not try cutting sandwiches or fruit into shapes using cookie cutters.
  Ingrid Powell, Hammondville, NSW.

- If including oranges in lunch boxes, score the rind in four sections with a knife. The skin will then pull off easily for little hands.
  Greta Cameron, Subiaco, WA.

- Make sure foods you pack for your kids are easy to eat. My kids are put off by fiddly packaging and don't like getting sticky hands.
  Katie Sherring, Fremantle, WA.

- I've got my kids in the habit of taking their lunch boxes into the kitchen straight after school so I can wash them and start filling them for the next day while preparing dinner.
  Joyce Wong, Darwin, NT.

- I do a big cook up once a month and freeze lunches – things like mini quiches, meatballs, cheese and Vegemite scrolls. And then I can put them straight into the lunch box from the freezer. It thaws ready for lunch time and makes life so much easier.
  Toni Mavis, via email.

HOME REMEDIES

HOME REMEDIES

HOME REMEDIES

- Try lip balm on a red nose when you've got a cold. It's soothing.
  Anna Duricek, Greystanes, NSW.

- Before you rip a bandaid off, dab it with vodka to help dissolve the adhesive and make it painless to remove.
  Anne Summers, Moonah, Tas.

- Buy a stethoscope so you can always listen to your heart.
  Louise Waldie, Helensvale, Qld.

- To get rid of nits, boil the pith of two limes. Cool and use to wash hair.
  R. Taylor, Glenview, Qld.

- To ward off head lice, give your child's hair a light spray of hairspray each day before school. It will coat the hair and lice won't be able to stick to it.
  Renee Chard, Marayong, NSW.

KATHLEEN TRIES IT OUT!

- To keep track of use-by dates on medications, highlight the dates with a texta.
Di Thomson, Bannockburn, Vic.

- To get rid of head lice, apply conditioner mixed with a few drops of eucalyptus oil and ½ teaspoon of tea tree oil, leave for 10 minutes. Comb hair and rinse.
Fiona Sio, Wyong, NSW.

- To help relieve itchy mosquito bites, soak cotton wool in white vinegar and dab over the affected area.
M. Nackovski, Mt Kembla, NSW.

- Try drinking turmeric and ginger tea to ease arthritis pain.
Mary Herman, Prospect, SA.

WACKY BUT IT WORKS

Carve your name into a potato and peel it as you picture yourself losing weight. Say to yourself, "I am slim, I am fit, I am getting rid of it!" Perform this potato ritual every time you feel tempted to overindulge.

HOME REMEDIES

- If you get a splinter, use sticky tape before resorting to tweezers or a needle. Simply put the tape over the splinter, and then pull it off.
Sheila McCarthy, Coobowie, SA.

- Try frozen ginger chips for soothing an upset tummy. Infuse fresh ginger in hot water. Strain, then freeze in ice-cube trays.
Grace Hoang, Cartwright, NSW.

You can heal paper cuts and immediately stop them stinging by applying lip balm to the area.
Chelsea Hartung, Liena, Tas.

- If you suffer from mouth ulcers, rub a small amount of Vegemite on them. It stings a little, but it cures them quickly.
W.Smith, Brisbane, Qld.

- Instead of using special seven-day tablet holders, I write Monday to Sunday on the packet. It's a free alternative and I never forget to take my pills now.
Janet Sutton, Ringwood, Vic.

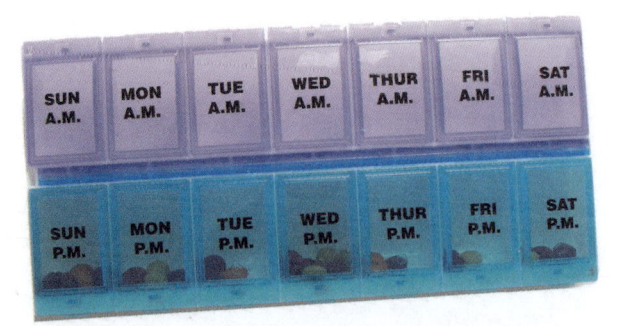

- To sooth itchy eyes, place two pre-brewed, cooled chamomile tea bags over your eyes for five minutes.
Maria Phillips, Wanneroo, WA.

- I find that cabbage leaves ease my joints when they get hot and painful. For best results I bind clean, slightly bruised leaves around the affected area and leave them there overnight.
  Meryl Pringle, Campbelltown, NSW.

- Swallow one to two teaspoons of sugar to get rid of hiccups fast!
  Louise Rawson, Deception Bay, Qld.

- Freeze aloe vera in an ice-cube tray for sunburn relief.
  Rex Graham, Five Dock, NSW.

- If you suffer from leg cramps, try drinking tonic water before you go to bed. The quinine in the drink acts as a muscle relaxant.
  R. Simpson, Wooloowin, Qld.

- Gargle six crushed garlic cloves mixed in a glass of warm water twice a day to cure a sore throat.
  Prudence Brennan, Matraville, NSW.

- To make a skin cleanser, cut a lemon in half and add four drops of honey on the top. Rub on your face for five minutes before rinsing off with cold water.
  Rebecca Guy, Norwood, SA.

HOME REMEDIES

- Because of my arthritis I find it hard to open doors, so I put a material bandage or Elastoplast around the doorknob and now it no longer slips out of my grasp.
Walter Moore, Glenelg, SA.

- To remove a splinter easily, apply a thick paste of baking soda and water, wait a few minutes and the splinter will pop out.
R. Stevenson, via email.

- If you are bitten by sand flies, dab white vinegar on the bite. It stops the itch almost instantly.
Lyman Gabaldon, Barmera, SA.

- Apply soap to a mosquito bite to stop itching.
Trudy Eleban, Darwin, NT.

- To help my son's allergy to dust mites, I add vinegar to my mopping water ($2/3$ cup per four litres). His sneezing has reduced since I started doing this.
Monica Johnson, Bathurst, NSW.

- Tea tree oil is a natural insecticide that helps to prevent and treat nits. Simply put two drops of tea tree oil into 60ml of fragrance-free shampoo and conditioner. Afterwards, thoroughly brush your child's hair with a fine-tooth comb.
Gabrielle Allwood, Ulladulla, NSW.

- Soak feet nightly in one part vinegar and two parts water to get rid of foot odour.
Regina Petrovic, Newtown, Vic.

KATHLEEN TRIES IT OUT!

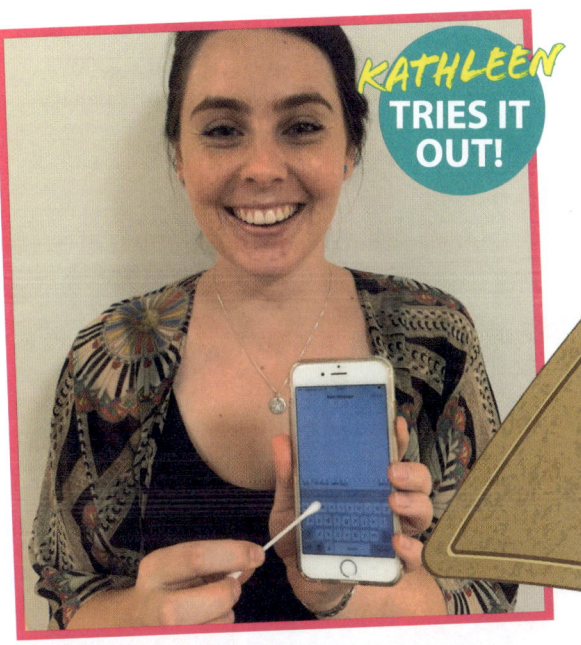

WACKY BUT IT WORKS

If you have clumsy fingers, type out your text on a phone using a cotton bud. It's so much easier.

- Gargle with a small cup of lemon juice to get rid of bad breath. It works!
  Paul Whelan, Dubbo, NSW.

- Rub olive oil into your lips a few times a day to soothe chapped lips.
  Bridie Marks, Blacktown, NSW.

- If your partner snores when on their back, put a tennis ball in a pocket cut from an old T-shirt and sew it to the mid-back of their pyjama top. They'll wake up when they roll over!
  Suzanne Krause, Palm Cove, Qld.

- To treat a bee sting, make a paste out of aspirin and water and apply to the sting.
  Renae Savidis, Moonah, Tas.

I add honey and lemon to my tea when I have a cold. I find it helps get rid of a cough, too.
Kylie Matthews, Brunswick, Vic.

HOME REMEDIES

227

WACKY BUT IT WORKS

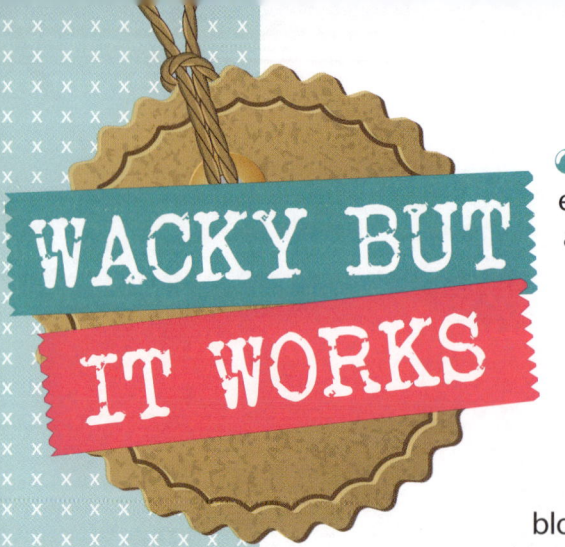

- If it gets icy outside, strap egg cartons to your elbows and knees to prevent injury if you fall.
Katie Cross, Warburton, Vic.

- No air conditioning at home or in your office on hot summer days? Simply strap a freezer block to an ordinary fan and enjoy the cool breeze.
Sammy Moss, Ararat, Vic.

KATHLEEN TRIES IT OUT!

- Scratched CDs or DVDs that don't work make colourful coasters for hot drinks.
R. White, Perth, WA.

- Rinse your hair with apple-cider vinegar to get rid of dandruff.
Lorraine Parkes, Belconnen, ACT.

- Make your own cereal by buying a box of cornflakes and mixing with your choice of fruit, nuts and rolled oats. This healthy breakfast will help keep your diet on track.
Kara Gilchrest, Young, NSW.

INDEX

A

airline tickets 108
allergies 208, 209
aluminium foil 195
ants 101, 150, 152, 179
apples 25, 69
apple cider vinegar 228
arthritis pain 223, 226
avocado 34

B

baby
    bottles 204
    change mats 213
    clothes 47
    crawling 201
    meals 214
    sleeping 206
    wipes 83
babysitting 170
bacon 31
bad breath 227
balloons 208
bamboo skewers 10
bananas 9, 10, 18, 31
    skins 145
Bandaids 127, 222
banking 112
barbecues 28, 36, 147, 148
bath cleaning 64, 78
bath toys 200
bathroom storage 91
batteries 162, 202
beanies 126
beauty tips 116–37
bed linen 93, 98

bedside table 101
bedwetting 202
bee stings 227
beeswax 118
beetroot stains 54
berries, storage 15
bibs 207
bicarbonate of soda 64, 65, 126
biro marks 53, 54, 58
birthday candles 187
birthday cards 165, 188, 203
birthday parties 203, 208
biscuits 8, 22, 73
bleach 72, 80
blenders 81
blinds 71, 83, 172
blood stains 53, 59
Blu-Tack 94
books 168
bookmarks 188
boots 137
bottle lids 8, 203
bottle openers 217
bras 123, 145, 182
brass pots 66
bread 9, 20, 169
bread clips 161
bronzer, chocolate 205
brooches 189
buckets 169
burning off 151
butter 8, 27, 36
    herb and garlic 20
buttermilk 31
buttons 49, 127, 129

INDEX

230

C

cake tins
- lining 9, 12, 30
- washing 8

cakes
- cutting 16, 37
- icing 14, 191
- storage 26
- transporting 26

calendars 165
cameras 196
camping 111, 112, 113
can openers 78
candle wax 82
candles 90, 95, 99, 187
cane furniture 94
capsicum 27
car grease stains 57
car parking guide 61
caravanning 113
cardholders 159

carpets
- deodorising 64
- stain removal 56

carrots 14, 33
- stain removal 54

cars 79, 82, 113, 151
- maintenance 160
- windows 151

caterpillars 154
cats 176–81
CDs 70, 96, 228
ceiling fans 81
celery 33
cereal 228
chalk 119, 123

chalkboard 213
chamois 85
charity donations 126
cheese 22, 34, 36
cheese graters 82
chewing gum 53, 206
child locks 213
child-proofing 200, 202, 204, 213

children
- cooking 213
- kids tips 198–219
- waking 183

chilling drinks 152
china, protection of 21
chocolate 25, 29
- 'bronzer' 205
- curls 20
- gift box 162
- melting 10
- strawberries 31

chopping boards 17, 66, 67
Christmas baking 99
Christmas decorations 60
chrome 57, 75
cleaner, abrasive 85
cleaning cloths 74
cleaning tips 64–86
clothes brush 47
clothes dryer 40, 47, 171
clothes drying 40, 41, 42, 43, 44, 46, 47
clothes mending 166
clove oil 76
cobwebs 84
coffee 10, 161, 168
- stains 52

collar stains 59
Colorbond 153
combs 80, 137
confetti 204
conversion chart 35
cook books 29
cooking oil 15, 152
cooling 98
copper pots 66
cork boards 96, 193
corn cobs 10, 11
cosmetic stains 57
coughs and colds 227
crackers 33
crawling babies 201
crayon marks 53, 82
crockery, stained 53
crystal 69
cucumbers 19
cupcake holders 11, 209
curtains 68, 80, 96, 98, 99, 161, 172
custard 18, 23
cuticles 131

D

decluttering 33
defrosting freezer 17, 20
deodorant stains 55
directions 166
discount coupons 108, 158
dishcloths 76
dishwashers 79, 173, 195
    tablets 158
dogs 176–81
    teeth brushing 176, 177, 178
doona covers 90
down-filled items, washing 45
drains, clogged 82, 154
drawers 90, 101
    dividers 212
dried flowers 70
dried fruit 25
drink bottles 208
drinks, chilling 152
dry shampoo 122, 137
    dogs, for 181
dry skin 128
dryer sheets 69
dust mites 226
DVDs 70, 96, 228

E

e-reader pouch 165
earrings 123, 129
egg cartons 211, 213, 228
egg cups 49
eggs 12, 13, 23, 21, 26, 31, 32, 37, 182
    shells 15, 140
electric blankets 94
energy conservation 169, 170, 172–3
entrance make-over 168
eskies 74
essential oils 91
eucalyptus oil 43, 46, 69, 76, 90, 179
exercise 195
exfoliating gloves 74

eye glasses 135, 146, 193
eyeliner 125, 130, 134
eyes, puffy 121, 127

F

face cleanser 120, 125, 135, 225
Facebook 85
fans 81, 181
fashion tips 116–37
fence stains 155
fertiliser 148
firelighters 143
fireplaces 73
fish scaling 142
fish tanks 81, 150, 164
flies 92, 94, 142, 143
floor tiles 73
flour, storage 12
flowers, cut 92, 95, 99, 186
foam sponges 11, 12, 159, 163
food colouring 15
foot odour 226
freezer 17, 20, 27, 173
freezer blocks 228
fridge 27, 65, 67, 173
fridge magnets 189, 204
frost protection 153
fruit, frozen 218
furniture
    assembling 194
    cleaning 54, 74, 93
    polish 77

G

games
    board 203
    children's 202, 205, 206, 207, 214
garage sales 168
garden tools 145, 153, 155
gardening 141–54
garlic 20, 26, 29, 130, 147, 148, 225
Gatorade 48
generic brands 171
gifts 162, 163, 164, 186, 191, 192, 194
ginger, fresh 22, 29, 224
glass, broken 71
glass/window cleaning 68, 70, 71, 85, 165
glass tables 71
glitter 200
glue/gap filler cartridges 94
glue tubes 189
goggles 183
gravy 24
grease stains 58
green vegetables 28
grey hair 121, 132
greywater recycling 146
grouting 72, 73, 78
gumboots, recycling 182
gutters 142

INDEX

233

H

hair 124
- brushes 80, 136, 137
- clips 129
- dye 122, 130
- grey 121, 132

hair lice 222, 223, 226
hairdressers 118, 128
hairnet 61
hairspray 48, 55
handbags 133
hand wash 129, 159, 165
hanging baskets 143, 151
hard drive, portable 188
hats 127, 128, 131, 170
heat ring marks, white 52
heels, soothing 124
hems 48
herb garden 153
herbs 15, 20
hiccups 225
hiding money 97, 159
highlighter stains 56
honey 18, 24, 148
hot water 169
hydration 131, 167

I

ice cubes 24, 216
ice cream 17, 217
ice cream cake 215
icepacks 11, 98, 121
icing cakes 14, 35
indoor plants 92, 93, 94

ink stains 53, 54, 58
insects 91, 92, 94, 101, 108, 121, 149, 150, 166, 228
insulation 173
interstate travel 109
invitations 188
ironing 40, 41, 43, 136
irons 72, 74
itchy
- bites 223, 226
- eyes 224

J

jeans 119
jewellery 76, 110, 119, 120, 123, 128, 131, 136, 137, 149
joint pain 225
juice, pouring 12

K

kettle cleaning 64
keyboards 186
keys 113
kids tips 198–219
kitchen bench space 30, 171
kitchen odours 65, 66, 77
kitchen tiles 84
kitchen tips 8–37
kitty litter 178
kiwi fruit 35
knee guards 145
knitting 193
knives 22

L

laminate stains 59
lampshades 80, 96, 100
lanterns 93
laptops 191
laundry tips 40–9
lavender 87–8, 91
lawns 147, 151
lazy Susans 32
leg cramps 225
lemons, juicing 17
lettuce, storage 24
light bulbs 90, 92, 94, 173
light switches 96
lint 122
lip balm 222, 224, 227
lip gloss 132
lipstick 137
    stains 48, 56
liquids, measuring 23
locks 91
lolly bags 205
loyalty programs 158, 161
lucky dip 207
luggage 110, 111
lunch boxes 60
    kids' 218

M

magnets 189, 204
    strips 193
magnifying glass 8, 32
make-up 121, 125, 130, 136, 137
    brushes 121, 131, 137
    marks 132
marble 84
material scraps 162
measuring liquids 23
meat, barbecuing 28
medicine
    children, giving to 211, 213, 215
    eye drops 216
    holder 224
memory boards 191
mending clothes 166
microwaves 75, 162
mildew stains 55
mint 36, 150
mirrors, bathroom 73, 79
moisturisers 119
money, hiding 97, 159
money saving tips 156–73
morning routine 118
moth holes 122
mouse traps 183
mouth ulcers 224
mushrooms 22

N

nail polish 118, 124, 126, 130, 132
    remover 133
name labels 216
necklaces 123
nits 222, 223, 226

O

off-peak travel 108
oil, disposal 19
online shopping 160, 169
oranges 25
outdoor furniture 140, 141, 150
outdoor rugs 141, 147, 204
outdoors tips 138–55
oven mitts 25
oven racks 65
ovens 76, 84

P

packing 111, 112, 114–15
paint, kids 200, 210
painting tips 100, 102–5, 155, 200
    oil-based, removal 54
palette planter 154
pancake batter 9
pancakes 216
pantihose 132, 133, 134
pantry moths 13, 21
paper cuts 225
parking guide 61
passwords 196
pasta 27, 65
    sauces 167
pastry 12, 23
patio tiles 144
pavers, stained 57
pegs, laundry 164
pencils, storage 213

pens 189, 193
    marks 53, 54, 58, 203
peppermint tea 30
permanent markers 53, 188
personal details 37
pet hair 45, 179
pet tips 174–83
petrol 160
petroleum jelly 54
pewter 67, 84
phones 49, 61, 183
    books 97
    chargers 173
photos 186, 195
    booth 203
picnics 142, 143, 147
pillowcases 41, 97, 120
pillows 42, 100
pincushion 190
piping bags 187
pitta bread 60
pizza cutters 32
plant cuttings 149, 150
planting 142, 144, 145, 146, 148, 149, 155
plastic bags 195, 197
plastic containers 14, 67, 80, 166, 167
polished floors 69, 85
poncho 167
pools 146, 153
possums 143
postage stamps 196
pot plants 146, 148, 150, 161
potatoes 9, 35
    jacket 11, 16

pots and pans 28, 32, 66, 77
pumpkin stain removal 54
puppy training mats 202

R

rangehood, cleaning 65
razors 124
receipts 135, 190, 195
recipes 190, 206
recycling 169, 209
red wine stains 52, 54
refrigerator seals 14
remedies, home 220–8
remote controls 61, 97
ribbons 188
rice
    coloured 212
    fried 113
rings 17, 136
rolling pins 18, 60
roses 144, 148
rubber bands 188
rubber washing-up gloves 19, 65
rubbish bins 64, 65, 152, 153, 155
rugs, outdoor 141, 147, 204
rust rings 72
rusty metal 52, 57, 58

S

sandpit toys 162
sandwiches 11, 33, 37, 161
sausages, barbecuing 36
sawdust 150
scarves 132, 134
scavenger hunts 207
school, first day 208
seedlings 146, 149, 164, 169
sensitive skin 125
sewing 194
shampoo 109, 122
shoe boxes 96, 134
shoes 79, 118, 120, 123, 124, 126, 127, 133, 136
    slippery 41, 119
shopping 167, 170, 194, 214
    online 160, 169
shoulder pads 129
shower curtains 68, 80
showers 80, 81, 84, 169
silverfish 121
silverware 67, 77, 84
sinks 66, 75, 76
skirting boards 71
slate floors 70
slugs and snails 140, 148, 150
smiles 134
snacks, kids 209, 210, 211
snoring 227
snorkelling goggles 183
socks 47, 78, 101, 132, 200
soft drinks, fizziness 8, 16, 33
solar lights 112
soup, freezing 34
spare coins 163, 167

spices, storage 28
spiders 45, 149, 182
splinters 225, 226
spring onions 21
stain removal tips 52–61
stainless steel, cleaning 55, 64, 78
steaming vegetables 23
sterilised water 80
sterilising jars 79
stethoscopes 222
sticky label marks 61, 66
sticky tape 48, 186
strainer, kitchen 49
strawberries 15, 17, 31
string, wrapping 197
stubby holders 148, 188
sugar 16, 18
sunburn 225
sundried tomatoes 36
sunglasses 202
sunscreen 171
sunshades 202

T

tackle boxes 197
taco shells 13
tea bags 13, 96, 109, 146
tea stains 52, 60
tea towels 13
tea tree oil 54, 64, 131, 226
television 165, 192
texting 227
thank you pebbles 197
thongs, rubber 183
throat, sore 225

Tic Tac boxes 192
tile grouting 72, 73, 78
to-do list 192
toasted sandwiches 11
toilet brushes 83
toilet training 204, 212
toilets 48, 72, 101
tomato paste 21
tomato sauce 34, 59
tomatoes 14, 23, 57, 142
toothbrush holder 95, 171
toothbrushes 67, 73
toothpaste 75
toothpicks 22
torches 147
towels 93, 98
toys 162, 200, 209, 217
train travel 110
travel tips 108–15
    children, with 108
    interstate 109
    pets, with 177, 180
trousers, hanging 43
tummy aches 224
tyre marks 151

U

umbrellas, wet 190, 197
unshrinking clothes 42
USBs 195

V

vacuum cleaner 101
vacuuming 80, 140
vases 141

Vegemite 49, 224
    jars 159
vegetable gardens 211
vegetables, steaming 23
Venetian blinds 71, 83
vinegar 43

W
wallpaper 97
walls 83, 99, 102, 177
wardrobes 68, 90
warranties 100
warts 125
washing 41, 42, 43, 45, 46, 83, 110, 172
    down-filled items 45
    powder 171
    woollens 46
    whites 43, 46
washing machine 43, 44
watches 120, 189
water
    conservation 158, 170
    drinking 131, 167, 201
water, flavoured 163
WD40 53, 133, 145, 206
weedkillers 144, 145, 152
wheel stops 100
wheelbarrows 141
white heat ring marks 52
whites, washing 43, 46
wholesalers 158
windows 68, 70, 71, 85, 165
wine 11, 31
wooden spoon 11
woollen underlays 45

woollens, washing 46
wrapping 187, 190, 192, 193, 194, 195, 197

X
X-rays 187

Z
zippers 191

Editor Paul Merrill
Deputy Editor Kate Kirsten
Designed by Angela Robins
Compiled by Danielle Sherring

A catalogue record for this book is available from
the National Library of Australia.
ISBN 978-1742459097
© Bauer Media Pty Limited 2016
ABN 18 053 273 546

This publication is copyright. No part of it may be
reproduced or transmitted in any form without the
written permission of the publishers.
Printed in China by Leo Paper Products Ltd

PUBLISHED IN 2016 BY BAUER MEDIA BOOKS, AUSTRALIA.
BAUER MEDIA BOOKS IS A DIVISION OF BAUER MEDIA PTY LTD.
Published by Bauer Media Books,
a division of Bauer Media Pty Ltd,
54 Park St, Sydney; GPO Box 4088;
Sydney, NSW 2001, Australia
Ph +61 2 9282 8618; Fax +61 2 9126 3702